# *The* POWER *to* APPREHEND

## *Dr. Debra A. Jordan*

## FOGHORN
PUBLISHERS
"Of Making Many Books There Is No End..."

The Power to Apprehend

Zoe Ministries
310 Riverside Drive
New York, NY 10025
www.prophetessdeborahjordan.com
www.bishopjordan.com

ISBN-10: 1-934466-10-7
ISBN-13: 978-1-934466-10-0
Printed in the United States of America

Foghorn Publishers
P.O. Box 8286
Manchester, CT 06040-0286
860-216-5622
860-568-4821 fax
foghornpublisher@aol.com

# Acknowledgements

*For the vision is yet for an appointed time,*
*but at the end it shall speak, and not lie:*
*though it tarry, wait for it; because it will*
*surely come, it will not tarry. Habakkuk 2:3*

I would like to thank all of the company of prophets, who for many years prophesied these books into my life. Each of these prophets skillfully saw into the heavens, each of the writings lying dormant within me, and commanded them to come forth. Thank you for your obedience to boldly declare the Word of the Lord concerning my destiny. Also, thank you for your patience in waiting for this gift to become a reality. To Dr. Aaron D. Lewis, for his publishing expertise, and his foresight to carry the seeds of my writings to the excellent finished product that you are holding. I would also like to thank Laurie Hicks for proofreading this work. Finally, I would like to thank all of my children, Naomi, Bethany, Joshua, Aaron, and Manasseh, who constantly encourage me in every way.

# Dedication

This book is dedicated to the two most influential men in my life, my father the late Charlie Berrian Sr. and to my husband Bishop E. Bernard Jordan. My father bequeathed to me, the special legacy of never giving up and always moving forward no matter what the circumstances. To my husband, Master Prophet Jordan whose ceaseless support never goes unnoticed. He always recognizes the very best in me. Both of these remarkable men are responsible for my spiritual development and growth. I am forever thankful for their greatness.

# Prophetic Partners

Carolyn Butts

Agnes Byrd, Prophetess

Ioana Beckford

Ramnarine & Patricia Petybaboo

Karlette Porter

Ruth Mclean

Tirzah Amafa

Anndera Peoples

Regina A. Croswell-Turner

Elexia Craig

Ovella Bilal

# Table of Contents

# Preface

The time and the season are ripe for the Church of the Lord Jesus Christ to grow up and begin to mature in the mysteries of Christ's Kingdom. It is time to come off the milk and begin to embrace the meat, the truths of God intended for maturing believers. For too long, the church has become comfortable sucking from the bottle of spiritually deficient pabulum. We have allowed believers to falsely suppose that their growth was somehow connected to attending events and functions, knowing all the lyrics to the most popular praise and worship songs, and following hard after celebrity preachers. They have successfully done all of those things; yet still remain shallow in their understanding of God, the world, and in their comprehension of esoteric themes in the Word of God.

In the midst of all of this confusion the "babes in Christ," continue to feed from the breasts of deception so long that these babies became grossly fat and unhealthy. They have become spiritually obese because they have not been given a proper diet to feed from. Most Christians know the antics of church, how to sing, dance, praise God, talk in tongues, and occasionally read their bibles enough to know all of the key scriptures most commonly mentioned. However, the vast majority of believers are spiritually immature, not having grasped the real concept of what it means to be a Christian or furthermore what it means to be Christ.

While the concept of being Christ has always been a very comfortable thought in the minds of the early Christians, modern Christianity denies any genuine connection to Christ. Most believers will readily deny that they are, or can ever become like Christ in this lifetime. While that train of thought may seem like an all too commonplace in most churches, in God's mind such thinking makes very little sense. Having been literally created in the image of God and in His likeness, your whole objective is to be like Christ. The best way to be like Christ is to simply be Christ. You cannot really separate one from the other.

*The best way to be like Christ is to simply be Christ. You cannot really separate one from the other.*

If what I am saying is a bit difficult for you to digest, it is only because you have yet to mature in the things of God such that these divine concepts will resonate within your soul and cause the war, or logic and reason to cease between your soul, spirit and flesh. Knowing who you are makes all of the difference in the world. This knowledge of self is a defining point in your life that will deliver you from being childish and needy to becoming God, the all sufficient One. In order to be like Christ you must first enter into His Kingdom.

However, the only ones who have access into the Kingdom of God are those who have an express function to carry out in the Kingdom of God structure. And that function must be carried with great humility and conviction. This simply means that your limited, parochial, or sectarian understanding must surrender to the all-encompassing knowledge of the mind of Christ. That which you think you know you must abandon so that you can open up your spirit to receive the truth concerning you, the truth of God.

> . . .*Verily I say unto you, Except ye be converted, and become as little children, ye shall not enter into the kingdom of heaven.*
>
> *Whosoever therefore shall humble himself as this little child, the same is greatest in the kingdom of heaven. Matthew 18:3–4*

The scripture tells us to be like a child or be as a child, not childish. This is conveying the message that all believers must have the redeeming traits of a child, such as forgiveness, love, humility, faith, and an eager willingness to learn. You must be like a sponge ready to absorb the Word of God whenever it is being served. Children are childlike, and that is good.

You too should be like a child. But you should not be childish, which implies that you have not grown up and are slowly retarding in your overall growth and development. You were not created to live a lifestyle of constant regression. You were created for movement, to move forward. By now you should be eating the meat of the Word, as the Apostle Paul suggested. But instead you are still getting your nourishment from the milk, the fundamentals that you embraced when you first became a believer. While that picture may look acceptable, it really is not. God expects you to grow, and to be able to digest more than the mere basics.

> *For when for the time ye ought to be teachers, ye have need that one teach you again which be the first principles of the oracles of God; and are become such as have need of milk, and not of strong meat. For every one that useth milk is unskilful in the word of righteousness: for he is a babe. But strong meat belongeth to them that are of full age, even those who by reason of use have*

*their senses exercised to discern both good and evil. Hebrews 5:12–14*

If you are not able to understand the mysteries of God today, when will you be? How long do you have to continually revisit the basics and repeatedly hear the same things over and again? At some point you should want to go beyond the learned behavior that has sought to enslave you. No longer should you accept for yourself the low requirements that the church has allowed you to live under.

If no one else will, expect more from yourself. You must move toward maturity. But in order to do that you must accept responsibility. Your spiritual development and growth is no one's duty to fulfill other than your own. In other words, you are responsible to make sure that you are getting the food that you need to sustain you, especially after you have spent years in the things of God, or should I say in the "things of the church?"

*...you are responsible to make sure that you are getting the food that you need to sustain you...*

Think about this in health terms. It is your responsibility to go to the doctor for your regular checkups and annual physical examination. If you do not go, then you may be jeopardizing a vital part of your health and maybe even your life. By simply making your appointment and keeping it, you greatly reduce the risk of sudden death. Even if you go to the doctor and get a negative report, it is still your responsibility to get a second opinion. Your doctor will not always tell you to do that, as he or she may believe that their care and diagnosis is sufficient.

When it comes to your spiritual survival you must do whatever it takes to ensure that you live and not die, regardless of who may not understand. This is not about motives.

This is about taking action when and where action is needed. This is about getting out of your comfort zone. Get away from sounds that you have always heard. Draw near to the fresh sound of new prophetic winds. One of the problems here is that it has become increasingly difficult to effectively gage who is growing in God from who is drowning in denial.

If the vast sea of churchgoers have been cloned to all look the same, and behave the same, the maturing saint, then becomes an oddball when he or she breaks out of the mode of tradition to become all that God has intended for them to be. More than that, they become an enemy of unfruitful thought. Beloved, you must become accepting of change. This is of God. You must be willing to be uncomfortable in order to experience the comfort of the Lord. Don't look for a place where everything that you hear, you feel comfortable with.

You will never grow in that place. You will only grow where you are hearing things that challenge your personal dogmas and cherished customs. In order to grow you must look for a prophetic voice that both cuts and heals at the same time. Once you find that person, stay there and grow strong under their voice. Immaturity always seeks to stay close to the person who only says what you want them to hear. You must move beyond that place. That is the land of irresponsibility and frivolity.

The longer that you run away from responsibility the more spiritually weakened you will be. The more that you embrace enlightenment the more you will grow and be given greater tasks to govern. Adam is a perfect example of this. When God created Adam, Adam initially embraced his responsibilities. Because of this, God gave him the reward for embracing more responsibility—dominion.

**do-min-ion**

-noun

1. the power or right of governing and controlling; sovereign authority.
2. rule; control; domination.
3. a territory, usually of considerable size, in which a single rulership holds sway.
4. lands or domains subject to sovereignty or control.

(Source: http://dictionary.reference.com)

The person who accepts responsibility will always be given dominion, they will be given something to rule over.

The person who does his or her job well will be elevated to a higher position, having control over more things. The reason why the church has not entered into her rightful place is because many leaders have become complacent leading mega-daycare centers instead of raising up disciples in the land to take authority.

*The person who accepts responsibility will always be given dominion, they will be given something to rule over.*

The church is swelling, she is fat, but yet not producing the kinds of fruit she was born to produce. The reason is that God does not allow babies to have dominion, only matured individuals. One of the signs of maturity is knowing to do what you are supposed to do without having to be told. For example, God never told Adam to go and name the animals in the garden. Adam named them because he intuitively knew that he was called to do so. He knew and understood that he was born to conquer, to be a doer, and to have dominion in the earth.

> *And out of the ground the LORD God formed every beast of the field, and every fowl of the air; and brought them unto Adam to see what he would call them: and whatsoever Adam called every living creature, that was the name thereof.*
> *Genesis 2:19*

Whatever comes from your ground, which is the soil of your mind, you have the right to name. God (the supernatural power and divine strength to make things come into being) will always come to see what you will call every experience you create. Everything that comes into your life, you created it with your own mind and thus have the authority to call it whatever you wish it to be. You name it. One of the greatest tragedies is when you fail to realize who you are and that God has called you to be a co-ruler with Him in the earth.

Adam had dominion in the earth until he abrogated his power and then gave it over to the serpent. The serpent's strategy has not changed in thousands of years. His simple stratagem is working more efficiently today than ever before. He convinces God's children that they are less than God. Once you fall into the trap of believing this lie, you will never be able to smell the sweet fragrance of greatness, living in the feeling of eternal inadequacy. Contrary to popular belief, the serpent rarely steals anything from the believer anymore. That was his former occupation.

Today many believers have made his job quite effortless by freely giving the serpent all of the things that God placed within our hands to control. We must move away from there. You must begin to develop confidence in the God within you. The first step toward this level of confidence is knowing that there is nothing on this earth that you cannot do. You must immediately remove the word "impossible" from your vocabulary, knowing that each time you utter such a venomous word that it grieves the heart of the Father by spewing out such blasphemy. The scriptures declare:

*I can do all things through Christ which strengtheneth me. Philippians 4:13*

*And he said, The things which are impossible with men are possible with God. Luke 18:27*

To believe anything other than this (these scriptural affirmations) is contrary to the nature of God. To believe other than this is to give more power to other gods than you give to your own self. Begin to refute the false concept that you are insignificant and that you cannot effectuate positive changes in your environment. God thinks about you all of the time. You have great significance in God's mind, and a special place in His heart. That is why God has entrusted you to govern all of the works of his hands.

*What is man, that thou art mindful of him? and the son of man, that thou visitest him? For thou hast made him a little lower than the angels, and hast crowned him with glory and honour. Thou madest him to have dominion over the works of thy hands; thou hast put all things under his feet. Psalms 8:4–6*

Within your mind lie great hidden treasures. You have the power to succeed. You have the power to get every job done that you set your hands to. The Greater One has made us unto Wisdom. Cooperate with the Spirit of God and come out from behind the walls of fear, the fear that you have erected with your own mind. Come out of your place of lethargy, from the arena of frustrated and unfulfilled purpose.

The church has wallowed in the sludge of inadequacy far too long. There is a beacon of light on the horizon that is powered by the greatness emanating from your life. You will not be a success, you already are. All things in Him are already done. It is up to you to discover the success within. It is time for us to arise collectively and go forth in the victory and the glory of God, and begin to seize one of the greatest hidden powers of all time—the power to apprehend!

> *Not as though I had already attained, either were already perfect: but I follow after, if that I may apprehend that for which also I am apprehended of Christ Jesus. Brethren, I count not myself to have*

*apprehended: but this one thing I do, forget-*
*ting those things which are behind, and*
*reaching forth unto those things which are*
*before. Philippians 3:12–13*

*Chapter One*

# The Call to Perfection

*Therefore leaving the principles of the doctrine of Christ, let us go on unto perfection; not laying again the foundation of repentance from dead works, and of faith toward God. Hebrews 6:1*

God is calling us to perfection. The whole idea of perfection has been misunderstood by many people, in that perfection is really not about being perfect in man's eyes. When God calls you to perfection, He is beckoning your soul to finish and complete that which you have started, or that which God started in you.

When you finish what God has begun in you, you make perfect His will and promises in the earth. Perfection, then takes on a different meaning than the meaning that is most commonly accepted. Jesus began an amazing work here on earth, and it is your job to finish what He started.

*God is calling us to perfection. The whole idea of perfection has been misunderstood by many people in that perfection is really not about being perfect in man's eyes.*

*Being confident of this very thing, that he which hath begun a good work in you will perform it until the day of Jesus Christ. Philippians 1:6*

God has given you the great mandate to occupy until He returns. Jesus said, *Occupy till I come. Luke 19:13.*

Consider the word, *occupy*. It is where we get our word *occupation* from, which means *to keep busy* or better yet, *to do profitable business*. God has blessed you to come to this earth to take care of important business. Remember that as long as you take care of God's business, He will take care of yours. Knowing this and accepting this as true will cause you to live a stress-free life. You really never lose sleep because you are too busy occupying.

People in the body of Christ need to understand that we are ambassadors for the King. When ambassadors enter a country, they are not affected by what is going on in that country. It doesn't matter if there is war, turmoil, and governmental unrest all around; the ambassador knows that the present condition of his or her own country is what matters most to them. If there is peace and rest in their land of citizenship then they too are peaceful and able to rest. However, if an ambassador from a particular nation visits a region where there is peacefulness, yet on the home front there is political and civil unrest, his soul will remain vexed even in a peaceful land, until his country becomes calm again.

Our citizenship is with the Kingdom of God or the Kingdom of Heaven on Earth. Our Lord is Christ. So whatever is going on in the King's life is also going on in ours as well. If the King is vexed then so are we. Theoretically speaking, if the King gets ill, then all of the citizens of that kingdom will remain ill too, until the King's condition becomes better. If the King is rich, then its citizens will feel rich and prosperous also, especially if the King has obtained His riches in an honorable fashion, not through exploitation and subjugating the people. Conversely if the King suffers from an impoverished state of mind, know well, that the citizens of that country will remain poor.

*...whatever is going on in the King's life is also going on in ours as well.*

Here is the update about the King. Great things are happening with the King, so great things should be happening in your life also. Are great things happening in your life? Are you moving from glory to glory? If you are, your lifestyle is reflecting the glory of the King. If you are not then you will need to adjust your ways to mirror the ways of God so that you will begin to receive all of the great benefits of belonging to this Kingdom. God's Kingdom is the image of perfection in the earth shown through His children.

This is very interesting, particularly since many people who claim to be Christians, do not reflect the image of Christ's perfection. Why is it that many Christians continue to suffer with sickness, disease, and think poor thoughts? Why is it that many people who do not profess to be Christians tend to lead a lifestyle where their needs are being met, and for the most part they are happy with how life is going? Why should anyone embrace Christ, after analyzing the life of most Christians who complain about everything and are obviously unhappy about where they are in life?

The believer's life should exemplify an aura of complete peace. Within that "complete peace" is the key to all prosperity. No peace no prosperity. Know peace and you will know prosperity. Your life should be one that reflects the glory of God. When your life illuminates with God's presence and glory, then you will be able to draw others to your experience in Him. However, that will only happen when you begin to embrace truths that are deeper and more solid than the truths that sustained you in your early years. You must move beyond milk.

*The church needs to have*
*just as high or higher*
*standards than the world.*

Many people fail to reach their highest potential in God, because they persist in holding onto the baby toys they were given at birth. The Word of God says, "It is time to grow up." In nearly every order, discipline, and field it is expected that you develop and grow in life. The church needs to have just as high or higher standards than the world. It is very unlikely that anyone will enter into the United States army as an E-1 private and remain at that same ranking some ten years later. By simply staying in the environment, the private will pick up on things here and there that will help him or her to advance in rank.

The church unfortunately has not developed the most effective system for developing the minds of its supporters. In fact for many leaders, developing their followers' minds is not even on their priority list of important things to do. It is not until your minds begin to become developed, and is stretched to its outer limits that you enter into a place of perfection. God expects more from you than what you have been displaying. You cannot use anyone or anything as an excuse, especially after reading these words. You are called to perfection.

You are expected to grow, develop, and mature into a totally new you. That will only happen as you not only begin to embrace new concepts about God, but you will also need to discard many of the old limiting beliefs that you have harbored for far too long.

Big, colorful, child-safe, plastic baby keys are a wonderful pastime for an infant. It provides them with temporary pleasure, helps them to explore colors, and gets them acclimated to touch sensitivity and shape recognition. That is great for babies. But imagine how worthless those same keys are to the person who needs new keys in life.

You cannot drive a Lexus or Mercedes Benz with baby keys. Baby keys will not open up the door to your new home. Those baby keys that you've held onto will not help you to have a solid marriage or healthy relationships in life. Those baby keys will not help you to be more profitable in business. So you must let the baby keys go. No matter how much you love those plastic keys, as you mature, you must trade them in for new keys that are far more relevant to the things that you need to do in life now. Even babies become dissatisfied with the same plastic keys after a few minutes or so.

They too begin to search for more satisfying and developmental tools that will sharpen their minds. That is a natural part of humankind. It is a supernatural function of the spiritual side in you. The child has an intuitive need to become more. That is why children get into so much mischief, because they are exploring. Children do not want to be in the same place for too long. They demand movement, and are born explorers, as you too should be. They are reaching for something bigger and more expressive than where they are right now. Let a child lead you by example. Begin to become completely dissatisfied with your present spiritual state, and insist on moving forward to a more glorious you.

## Making the Right Choice

*And there were four leprous men at the entering in of the gate: and they said one to another, Why sit we here until we die? If we say, We will enter into the city, then the famine is in the city, and we shall die there: and if we sit still here, we die also. Now therefore come, and let us fall unto the host of the Syrians: if they save us alive, we shall live; and if they kill us, we shall but die. And they rose up in the twilight, to go unto the camp of the Syrians: and when they were come to the uttermost part of the camp of Syria, behold, there was no man there. For the Lord had made the host of the Syrians to hear a noise of chariots, and a noise of horses, even the noise of a great host: and they said one to another, Lo, the king of Israel hath hired against us the kings of the Hittites, and the kings of the Egyptians, to come upon us. Wherefore they arose and fled in the twilight, and left their tents, and their horses, and their asses, even the camp as it was, and fled for their life. And when these lepers came to the uttermost part of the camp, they went into one tent, and did eat and drink, and carried thence silver, and gold, and raiment, and went and hid it; and came again, and entered into another tent, and carried thence also, and went and hid it. 2 Kings 7:3–8*

At times you will find that making the right choice in life requires simply making a choice and sticking to it. Here in these passages of Scripture we find that the four lepers made a qualified decision. They looked at their situation and realized that there was no way out no matter what avenue they chose. If they went into the city they would have been killed had they been caught. If they chose to stay were they where they would have died from starvation. The famine was so great in the land that they really would not have been able to survive there.

If someone had food they probably would not have shared their food with the lepers seeing that the society in which they lived, considered them as dead anyway. The way that most people thought then was, "Why bother wasting food on four men who were not really making a difference in society?" Lepers did not have a chance at surviving, especially during tough times. They were at the top of the list of social outcasts. Interestingly these lepers made up in their mind that it would be better to become captured by the Syrian army. If there was any such thing as a chance, this was their only one. The immortal words *"Why sit here till we die?"* has become the catch phrase of choice for people determined to take action in life and refrain from excuse making.

If inactivity produces little to nothing in life, then taking action will obviously produce more favorable results. Why sit here till we die? The mature believer realizes that God is calling us to take action. The book of Acts is an entire book dedicated to the Acts or actions of the apostles. In this book we can find several examples of how God gave favors to those people willing to take immediate action, even against the odds. The old folks used to say,

"If you take one step, God will take two." God will move supernaturally in your life when you choose to take a step in the right direction, when you do something that you've never done before, something that requires faith.

Making a quality choice has much to do with acting responsibly. Acting in faith is acting responsibly. Some people put the entire load on God in such a way as to opt themselves out. That is not responsible. You must be willing to take action. Your actions have more to do with your miracle than you actually realize. Your faith, and your actions begin to work things out for your good. God in you, working with your faith in action, produces a synergistic effect in the universe causing everything that you think to become a manifested reality. This process begins once you make the right choice, to choose.

If making the right choices, or even choosing to choose is so valuable in life, why aren't more people doing it? Whether in secular society or in the church world people tend to be loyal to traditions that limit them from being able to make choices. If making the right choice means that you must go against the status quo in life, or that you must appear contrary to the established norm, most people choose not to choose. Another reason people choose not to choose, is because they are very much like slaves who have been under the rule of the master for so long that they cannot seem to make a concrete decision without the master's approval.

We see this often in society within our welfare system, which is another form of modern day slavery. The system makes all of the choices for you. They choose where you live, what you eat, and where you can or cannot go to school. To make the choice to do anything outside of the establishment makes you become a demagogue since we are trained to allow others to choose for us. The problem here is that if you do not make the right choices in life, for yourself, you will never grow up. Also, when you do not make the right choices in life you will always live a life of compromise, knowing that you could do more, be more, and have more, but rather choosing to do nothing instead.

*The system makes
all of the choices for you.*

*They choose where you
live, what you eat, and
where you can or cannot
go to school.*

*If you limit your choices only to what seems
possible or reasonable, you disconnect yourself from what you truly want, and all that
is left is a compromise. —Robert Fritz*

This is why your perfection in Christ comes with the burden
of responsibility. As you grow up in God, you become more
value conscious. You begin to make decisions based on
your values and principles. Babies don't have values
because they are always being taken care of. Children
particularly have the values of their parents, since that is
their only example. Slaves only have the values of their
master. If they choose to have different values than their
master, their master will quickly correct them, because
having a different set of values means that the master's

values is no longer singularly unique. That puts the master's system in jeopardy.

But it is only when you embrace those things that God speaks to your heart that you mature in Him because that's what will produce a cleansing, purging, and fire effect. And that is what this work is all about. This is about getting you to make the choices to begin to think differently than you ever have before and acting on those new thoughts in your mind. Remember it doesn't have to feel, look, or smell, like the former things in order to be God. The immature believes that God is only doing what He has already done before. The mature knows all too well, that God is doing a new thing in the earth, and is eagerly awaiting the demonstration of His power.

> *Behold, I will do a new thing; now it shall spring forth; shall ye not know it? I will even make a way in the wilderness, and rivers in the desert. Isaiah 43:19*

When you were a baby, your mother or care provider, changed your diapers, fed you three times daily, and washed you and sang lullabies to you at night. That phase ended only when you matured into another level of life, which resulted in your making choices. You made the choice to explore areas like touching things that you weren't supposed to touch in an effort to learn more about life. Through trial and error you learned how to respect things like fire and water.

You knew not to break the television, or CD player, because you knew there were consequences in doing so. That was your process toward maturity. You made choices and those choices brought you to a new level of maturity. Many believers are spiritually retarded because they have not made any new life advancing choices since they received Christ. The truth of the matter is that as you become perfected in God, you will make not just a few choices, but many.

Don't try to second-guess yourself. Do not try to qualify every choice. That will only frustrate you and make your process seem arduous. Some of the choices that you make will not always turn out the way that you initially thought they would. The important thing is that you never stop making choices in life. The more choices that you begin to make will navigate you closer to the place in God that you truly desire, making your spiritual worth increase. Don't avoid the fire and pressure associated with making choices; it's the only way to become gold.

> *And I will bring the third part through the fire, and will refine them as silver is refined, and will try them as gold is tried: they shall call on my name, and I will hear them: I will say, It is my people: and they shall say, The LORD is my God. Zechariah 13:9*

## Let Go of What's Holding You Back

> *Wherefore seeing we also are compassed about with so great a cloud of witnesses, let us lay aside every weight, and the sin which doth so easily beset us, and let us run with patience the race that is set before us. Hebrews 12:1*

In order to go forward you must embrace the Law of Release. What you are willing to let go of in life will determine what will come into your life. That which you hold onto tightly will eventually evaporate. It will whist away. You can look at this law in this manner, what you release will cause the action of an equal or greater blessing to be released into your life again. When you refuse to let go of the weight, the weight, which you are holding onto too tightly, will eventually destroy you. It will become too heavy for you to bear.

*In order to go forward you must embrace the Law of Release. What you are willing to let go of in life will determine what will come into your life.*

You cannot run a race carrying too much baggage; you will have to release the weight so that you can run well without any hindrances or encumbrances. Soldiers typically travel light. In antiquity, the heaviest thing that soldiers would carry was their armor and sword for protection.

Other than that they would not carry anything else, as carrying too much weight would hinder their effectiveness when fighting the enemy. It's no different with you. The enemy in your mind can easily be defeated as soon as you choose to eliminate the petty things that you've allowed to become more important than it actually is.

Those things have held you back in life. Just let it go! This is all about coming into maturity and perfection. Just think about when you were much younger, how certain things used to disturb you, make you angry, or even act irrationally. Now those same things don't even faze you. You simply ignore them. Why is that? You realize that those things were nothing more than weights that didn't really serve a meaningful purpose. You are growing up. You are more mature now than you were then. And you are more focused on the reality that you have a job to complete and a mission to fulfill. You are being made perfect in Christ. So those things no longer have a hold on you. Thank God!

*Since we have such a huge crowd of men of*
*faith watching us from the grandstands, let*
*us strip off anything that slows us down or*

*holds us back, and especially those sins that*
*wrap themselves so tightly around our feet*
*and trip us up; and let us run with patience*
*the particular race that God has set before*
*us. Hebrews 12:1 TLB*

The Living Bible translation has a rather interesting outlook on this Scripture. The sins that beset, offset, and upset us wrap themselves tightly around our feet causing us to stumble and trip. This is why God requires of all of us to live a lifestyle exercising patience. Without patience our race will be ineffective. You will never win without patience. But patience is only for the mature person in God not babies. So you must first have a willingness to wait. Anything that will ever have lasting value in life was made, tested, and tried over time. Nothing great ever happens overnight.

It doesn't matter whether this thing is a church, a business, a marriage, a friendship, or ever the value of a stock, the strength and enduring quality of that thing will be determined in its ability to wait-it-out. Sometimes when I hear pastors talk about how they started a church today and one month later they are boasting two thousand members, my heart goes out to them.

Although, I would never want to crush their precious spirit, I know that they've only created a cockatrice so big and ugly that will have to be dealt with at the most inopportune time, and when they least expect it. Being enamored with the idea of greatness, and measuring greatness by the measuring stick of fast growth can be grossly deceiving. And when the thing that has grown so large, proceeds to eat you alive—that is when you suddenly begin to wish that you had only spent more time with that thing, to determine what it was capable of doing. Knowing people and understanding their motives only comes through time spent with them, which requires much patience.

*Patience is what builds strong institutions and causes them to last. There is nothing wrong with growth.*

*But growth that comes*

*too quickly can be*

*very dangerous.*

Patience is what builds strong institutions and causes them to last. There is nothing wrong with growth. But growth that comes too quickly can be very dangerous. Imagine if your three year old began to eat so much fast food, that when he or she finally weighed they were more than 100 pounds. Something would be very wrong about this. Growth isn't bad; but a 100 pound three year old is very unhealthy. The things that we need to know about God will never come through one bible teaching. Your growth will come through the consistent and focused attention to His Word throughout life, not just a few power sessions.

There are some teachings that the masses cannot participate in, but are reserved for the few disciples who have proven to be faithful students of the spirit. In most churches the Bible study is open to all. When the study is open to all, you must continually teach remedial lessons over and over, as not to offend or confuse the newborn lambs. The problem is that many of the little lambs have grown up but are still feeding off of lamb chow carefully designed for newborns. Developing the mind is a lifelong journey, and it will take much staying power to become what God has intended you to be. The good thing is that every bit of time invested into developing your mind is totally worth the wait.

*There are some teachings*
*that the masses cannot*
*participate in, but are*
*reserved for the few*
*disciples who have proven*
*to be faithful students*
*of the spirit.*

So the first area of concern is your resistance with patience. The second concern is equally as self defeating— your willingness to let go. Every great runner wears very lightweight sneakers, shorts, and a tank top while training and competing. Sometimes they wear a body suit, especially made for the sport. Whatever they choose, it is always light-weight. The runner realizes that their speed and accuracy comes through having only what they need, nothing more. There are so many things that you can trim from your life. Certain friends, some new or old acquaintances, and old ways of thinking are all things that once shed from your life will cause you to take off running in the things of God.

Stop holding on to dead, old, non-working traditions. It doesn't matter if it was good enough for your mom and dad, or your grandparents; obviously it is not good enough for you. So let it go. Let go of those friendships that are draining. They are going nowhere. Let go of the family members who constantly berate you and spew out accusations and false rumors against you. Dr. Mike Murdock says, "Go where you are celebrated, not tolerated." You must not subject yourself to an arena of people who do not value where you are going.

*Stop holding on, to dead, old,*
*non-working traditions.*

Some people can only handle where you have been in life, but not where you are going. As tough as it may be, you are going to have to let them go. The place that God has prepared for you is too precious to forfeit in exchange for meaningless rubbish. Taking stuff off, and letting go helps you to run faster. The enemy of your mind makes you falsely believe that you need a crowd in order to get the job done. But that isn't true. You, God and the few others that He has assigned to your life are fully capable of helping you to complete your assignment.

*Some people can only handle*
*where you have been in life, but*
*not where you are going.*

I've been told that the way to achieve your goals in life is through concentrated focus. I suggest to you, that you begin to focus more than ever before on the place that God has prepared for you, the place that He has shown you in your soul. What kind of place is it? Is it lovely? Is it a place of peace and prosperity? Does the Spirit of God reign freely there? If this place is as good as you envision it to be, then you must let go of anything that may delay your process in getting there.

> *In my Father's house are many mansions: if it were not so, I would have told you. I go to prepare a place for you. And if I go and prepare a place for you, I will come again, and receive you unto myself; that where I am, there ye may be also. And whither I go ye know, and the way ye know. John 14:2–4*

Remember that in order to become perfected in God and come into the place of maturity you must:

- Practice the art of patience, learn and grow through this practice.

- Quickly release anything in your life that is not adding to you, but rather slowly draining you of your ability to "grow forward."

## Can You Handle It?

*For my yoke is easy, and my burden is light. Matthew 11:30*

God will never ever give you more than you can handle. But He will always put you in a position where you will be stretched and sometimes to the max. He does that because he knows you can handle it. Also, God does that because it stretches your faith. Just when you think that you've had enough, God steps in and gives you more to handle. Sometimes you feel as if you are not going to be able to make it, but you will. The good thing is that God only gives you according to your ability.

*God will never ever give you more than you can handle.*

*But He will always put*

*you in a position where*

*you will be stretched and*

*sometimes to the max.*

*And unto one he gave five talents, to another two, and to another one; to every man according to his several ability; and straightway took his journey. Matthew 25:15*

As you grow in the knowledge of God and begin to understand how God relates to and chooses people to complete certain kingdom tasks, you will realize that God only gives a person what they can handle. One of the faults of leaders is that we often assume that every person has the same abilities and can handle the same kinds of responsibilities. This is not true. As simple as one task may be to you, it may be complete drudgery to the next man or woman. Some people love to write; others absolutely hate it, and need to employ the services of one who can help them to translate their thoughts onto the paper, making them permanent.

God calls some people to speak publicly, and when you watch them, you are amazed by how easily they flow with their words. There are some people who dread the thought of speaking in front of an audience, choosing death over speaking. This is not to say that a person cannot be developed in this gift. I have seen many times even in our ministry how different people came into perfection, learning how to speak better, or administrate better, or even serve better. They did this because we were patient with them, and they were also patient with the process involved.

However, there were times when we invested an enormous amount of time in certain people and they just couldn't get it. They were not able to grasp the challenge of being able to do what was asked of them. We had to just face it. They were not able to do it. The quicker that leaders identify or discern what a person is really able to do, the less time they will waste. You too must be able to be honest about the things that you are not inclined toward. To become perfected in God you must not spend too much time in the wrong area.

Imagine a person in New York trying to get to Los Angeles, but they are driving toward Connecticut, no matter how hard they try to get to California, it just won't happen, because they are exerting energy in the wrong direction. Perfection in Him is not about making a whole lot of movement; it's about doing what you are able to do, and doing it until you see the desired results.

## Chapter Two

# Faith Without Works Is Dead

We serve a God who will not only supply your needs, but who will also grant you the desires of your heart. God doubles what you need from Him. God is a multiplier and increaser. Whatever He touches it has to become more than what it was before He touched it. That is the very nature of God. When God touches your finances, your finances have to increase. There are no other alternatives. If God touches the lives of your progeny, your children will have to increase—they will have to become more than what they were to begin with.

God is a God of increase. And in the same manner that God increases whatever he touches, He expects you to do exactly the same. Every institution that God ordains is one that He expects "increase" to be the by-product. In marriage, every wife should increase or double her husband. If she does not double him then she is not fulfilling her optimum role as a wife and a helpmeet. If she reduces him or causes him to live a lifestyle of utter embarrassment and shame, then she has not performed her function as a wife. The same concept goes for the man who is also required to double his wife.

However she came into the marriage, it should be the husband's primary concern to ensure that his wife becomes more than what she was. This same concept holds true for the children as well. Every child should double his or her parents by bringing honor to their name. That is why parents need to invest so much in their children, because everything that they invest will come back to them multiplied. Every employee should double their employer by causing their place of work to become far more productive than it has ever been before. By following God's lead one can easily see how we will have a more fruitful and productive life. You must live your life seeking areas where you can double others.

*Every child should double*
*his or her parents by*
*bringing honor to*
*their name.*

How can you increase the lives of others and your own life? The pathway to more is through faith and action. As you mature in God you will discover that your faith in God and even your faith in the God inside of you, which is faith in yourself, will lead you into realms unimaginable. Faith is your ticket to experience anything that you desire. The issue with faith is that far too few believers actually walk in faith, because they have not taken the time to become mature in their most holy faith. Faith is not something that can be easily recognized at first glance. You must develop faith.

Today most people use digital cameras to take photographs. Before there were digital cameras there were cameras that required a roll of film. Before you could see the image on the film you would have to take the film to a processor and get it developed in the darkroom. This analogy is very pertinent to your life and where you may be right now. It may seem like a dark moment in your life right now. However, it is in the darkness that God develops you into His most beautiful workmanship. In the darkness your faith is developed. The images in your life to others may seem very strange, and at times almost indescribable as you are dealing with situations day to day.

People may look at where you are today, and believe that is where you will be for the rest of your life. That is not so. Tell those people to wait just a little while longer, and keep looking. Tell them to keep observing. Right before their eyes, they will see you developing into something that looks totally different than how you looked before. God desires to develop your faith. The way that God does this is by allowing you to live within chaos, so that He can say, "Let there be." God wants you to live in a state where your earth, which is you, is without form and is void, and all around you is darkness.

*And the earth was without form, and void;*
*and darkness was upon the face of the deep.*
*And the Spirit of God moved upon the face*
*of the waters. And God said, Let there be*
*light: and there was light. Genesis 1:2–3*

Unlike anyone, anywhere, at anytime in history, God alone
will host a great celebration especially for you, while you
are in darkness. Contrary to popular belief, God celebrates
your darkness. Often in Christianity, we have heard people
try to connect your darkness with sin and licentious living.
This is not true. The Bible speaks of Job who was a man
who was perfect and upright, and one that feared God, and
eschewed evil. He did all of the right things, honored God,
and led a lifestyle of high integrity. Yet despite Job's obvious
commitment to God, he faced one of the darkest days of his
life, losing all of his possessions, his family, and his friends.

*Contrary to popular belief, God*
*celebrates your darkness.*

Job became extremely ill throughout the course of this dark time in his life, yet he still knew intuitively that God in himself would deliver him to an entirely new existence. How did he maintain his sanity in this dark hour? Job worked his faith by developing it during hard times. The most important season in your life is not your season in the light, but rather your season in darkness. Darkness develops your inner character unlike anything else. Church people may tend to criticize you and berate you because you are going through one of life's storms. Don't worry about that.

God smiles when you are going through darkness, because He knows that He has equipped you with everything that you will ever need on the inside of you to come out victoriously. The atheists falsely believes that religion and believing in God is designed for you to fail in life, and that He is the originator and perpetrator of all societal ills, such as widespread hunger and disease, genocide, ethnic cleansing, and many other evils. They believe that if God were indeed a good God that these things would not exist. The truth of the matter is that God is a good God. In fact, God is great, so great that He caused you and I to become the solution to the ills in the world and for the world. We are the answer. The Christ in us is the answer for life's problems.

*God is great, so great that*
*He caused you and I to*
*become the solution to the*
*ills in the world and for the*
*world. We are the answer.*

So then, whatever problem exists on earth, we are here to solve it. The only reason that these problems continue to persist is simply because believers and non-believers have abrogated their roles in the land, idly waiting for God to do something. Whatever your desire may be: increased passion for humanity, to be a philanthropic giver, to cure AIDS, or to bring about world peace and end all wars, He has already given you the power to succeed. All you have to do is tap into your faith.

*May he give you the desire of your heart*
*and make all your plans succeed.*
*Psalms 20:4 NIV*

The blessings of the Lord don't discriminate with respect to race, creed, sex, or even age. The thing that activates God's blessing and His lavish favor upon your life is faith. As long as you are willing to actively engage in God's business, He will equip you to fulfill the job no matter how old or young you are. On one occasion, when Jesus was a child, His parents went looking for Him, having been missing in action for three days. When they finally found Him, instead of apologizing to His parents for causing them worry, He told them that He was somewhere busy doing His Father's business. The story is recorded in Luke chapter 2.

*And it came to pass, that after three days*
*they found him in the temple, sitting in*
*the midst of the doctors, both hearing*
*them, and asking them questions. And all*
*that heard him were astonished at his*
*understanding and answers. And when*

*they saw him, they were amazed: and his mother said unto him, Son, why hast thou thus dealt with us? behold, thy father and I have sought thee sorrowing. And he said unto them, How is it that ye sought me? wist ye not that I must be about my Father's business?*

*Luke 2:46–49*

The phrase wist ye is a Greek verb typically used in past tenses, but perhaps taken somewhat indignantly here. It's almost as if the young Savior was challenging their minds by implying, "Why didn't you know that I was doing my Father's business, wasn't it obvious?" Of course I am paraphrasing here, but this is definitely the tone that is being implied here. How is it that a young Jesus can have so much confidence and courage to stay away from His parents for three days, and not worry for his life, or care about His parent's reaction? Jesus understood at a very young age that maturity in the things of God has very little to do with age, but rather the ability to exercise faith as often as possible.

*God recruits both the young and the old, as He has specific assignments for both of them that are custom tailored to their peer group.*

It doesn't matter how young you are, God will use you mightily if you are open to change and willing to walk the walk of faith. God recruits both the young and the old, as He has specific assignments for both of them that are custom tailored to their peer group. He calls the old to reach the old, and the young to reach the young, and the extraordinary to influence the extraordinary. Like always begets like. Simply activating your faith does all this. Jesus astounded the doctors and other learned men in the temple by releasing His faith to do the unexpected. The mature believer must always increase, and in doing so, they must do something that is totally unexpected. This is a true sign of a maturing spirit.

For example if you have been giving $20, or $50 for the past ten years, and that is the highest that you will give today, then you are not maturing because you are doing only what is expected. You are giving in the area of your comfort zone. This is why vowing unto God is so vitally important because you vow amounts of money that people would not expect you to vow. You must serve in areas where people wouldn't normally see you serving. Why is this? You must come out of you area of ease and release your faith by doing something that you have never done before. The young are doing it, and so are the old. Consider Abram, when he was in his senior years, how God told him to relocate to a totally strange land.

> *Now the LORD had said unto Abram, Get*
> *thee out of thy country, and from thy kindred,*
> *and from thy father's house, unto a land*
> *that I will shew thee: And I will make of*
> *thee a great nation, and I will bless thee,*
> *and make thy name great; and thou shalt*

*be a blessing: And I will bless them that bless thee, and curse him that curseth thee: and in thee shall all families of the earth be blessed. So Abram departed, as the LORD had spoken unto him; and Lot went with him: and Abram was seventy and five years old when he departed out of Haran. Genesis 12:1–4*

Imagine this, Abram was at an age when most people are looking forward to retirement, but instead he is getting re-fired to do something unexpected—move to a new land. Why didn't God tell Abram to move to the neighborhood down the street, or two towns over? God told Abram to get out of his country, and get away from his family. The strong implication here is that there are some places where your blessings will be limited because that place is too familiar to you, and so are the people around you. God told Abram not to move in with his family, but rather to get away from them. Does God not promote the idea of strong and loving families? Of course God believes in family.

God knows though, that family are oftentimes the worst people to expose yourself to, especially when you are becoming more than what you were before. The blessing and favor, which was to come on Abrams life, was so magnificent that his family may not have been able to handle it, so God had to get him move far away from any potential disturbances or setbacks. His age did not matter. The only thing that really matters in your faith walk is your willingness to obey when God says go, and when God says let. Will you go when God says go? Will you *let* God? The answer to those questions will determine the quality of the rest of your life.

*The only thing that really matters in your faith walk is your willingness to obey when God says go, and when God says let.*

## Work Your Faith

Faith is always looking for work. Or should I say God is always looking for someone to work his or her faith. This is the only way that God gets pleasure, and it is the only way that the believer will ever grow into maturity. One thing that produces spiritual retardation is by not embracing higher truths concerning God, as I alluded to in the previous chapter. Something that produces that same level of retrogression is when you fail to embrace opportunities to live by, exercise, and act in faith. The strangest thing is that many people who claim to walk with God, at times use less faith than the people who oppose the things of God. That has never made much sense to me.

I've always been amazed by business people who do not admit to having a relationship with God, yet exercise extraordinary faith in the universe and in themselves to create massive portfolio and passive incomes. While God desires to have a loving relationship with all His children, He cannot ignore the ones who are consistently showing up to the table to do amazing things, things that have never been done before. As a young adult in church, I would often hear the preacher criticize the sinner, and condemn them. But if the truth were told, many sinners exercise far more faith than believers do. Perhaps this is why God within them is continually rewarding them with their hearts desire. Remember, God is no respecter of persons, but He is and always will be a respecter of faith. And God gives those who act in faith His ability to continue to do so.

*... many sinners*
*exercise far more faith*
*than believers do.*

*What does it profit, my brethren, if someone*
*says he has faith but does not have works?*
*Can faith save him? If a brother or sister is*
*naked and destitute of daily food, 16 and*
*one of you says to them, "Depart in peace,*
*be warmed and filled," but you do not give*

*them the things which are needed for the body, what does it profit? Thus also faith by itself, if it does not have works, is dead. James 2:14-17 NKJV*

Faith as defined by Strong's Concordance means to persuade or being persuaded, a belief, confident in the divine truth. In order for you to have faith, you must first be persuaded and confident in the divine truth that you profess to know. You must know God, but not the God in outer space. You must know the God who dwells inside of you. In order to boldly take action in faith you must know the truth as truth and you must know the truth as yourself. What is the truth? The truth is that the only God that there is is the one who dwells on the inside of you. That is why when you pray you must pray from within, not from without.

*When you meditate on the thoughts inside of you, the God who lives inside of you*

*creates the thoughts and*
*makes them a manifested*
*reality in your life.*

When you meditate on the thoughts inside of you, the God who lives inside of you creates the thoughts and makes them a manifested reality in your life. You took the time to work the thoughts that were on the inside of you, by taking action toward the idea in your mind. The word *work* means *a performance*. It also denotes any matter, thing, or object, which one may have to do. *Work* can also mean *attainment* or *realization of an accomplishment*. So when you are genuinely working, you are working toward something. Your subconscious mind is taking you somewhere that your faith would like to explore.

Faith without works, which means *being persuaded of a belief in the divine truth without attaining what you are persuaded of* is dead, or produces death. *Dead* is defined as *inactive and inoperative*. Dead faith is that faith which is not able to sustain you in your day of visitation. Dead faith is that kind which does not last long enough to actualize the benefits so true faith cannot really exist at all, unless works accompanies it. If someone claims to have faith, yet does nothing, then that person is deceived. All genuine faith is accompanied by works, and corresponding actions, which always causes the individual to realize the object of their faith.

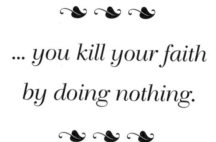

*... you kill your faith*
*by doing nothing.*

Let's look at it this way: You kill your faith by doing nothing. When you do that often enough, you will eventually kill yourself in the process. Have you ever heard someone claim to believe in divine health? They'll say, "I believe God. I know that God wants me to prosper and walk in divine health." They know this in word and in theory but not in deed. Just knowing something in word will never afford you the blessings associated with the words. You will only touch greatness when you combine the knowledge of your words with actions. The same people who believe that God wants them to enjoy optimal health will: eat all of the wrong foods, snack on junk food with low nutritional value, or even eat highly fattening foods late at night.

They are doing the total opposite of what they are professing to believe, and what will produce good health. If you are claiming that you are walking in perfect health, yet violate dietary laws, and avoid exercise, then your faith has no works in demonstration. You can say all day long "God wants me to be healthy." It means nothing at all. Those are just empty words until you actually do something about it, until you take action. I've heard people say "Money cometh to me now," yet they are still broke, busted, and disgusted. Many people expect that when they make such confessions that God is going to rain down money from the sky. This is not how God works.

When you confess wealth and riches, it is only the beginning. Saying it is the start. By saying it, you are cultivating the environment in which rich soil is produced. But after the soil is produced nothing will grow from it, until you plant a seed in faith. You have to do something. In general, wealthy people own or lead businesses. So if you are really going to be wealthy you must move toward that intended goal of beginning your business, moving some type of good, product, or service. So what if you fail at your first attempt. The very act of acting actually releases a heavenly mixture in you that will cause you to continue to knock on many doors until the right one eventually opens for you.

You have got to get up and do something. The late great Hammond B-3 organist and music extraordinaire Billy Preston said in his song, "Nothing from nothing, leaves nothing." Millions of people sang that song, tapped their feet to the tune, but yet did not really catch the powerful and prophetic message being sent forth. Like God told Abram, God is telling you to step out of your comfort zone and do something totally out of character, something totally unlike you, that will yield heavenly results.

**The Treasure Inside of You**

Knowledge is good and it is powerful, but it must be used the right way. You can have whatever you desire, you can be whatever you dream of being, and you can do whatever your soul chooses to do. But before you can receive any of those things you must be very intent on what it is that you want for yourself. The answer to your divine desires is living inside of the treasure within your body.

The world that we live in is desperately seeking out spirituality, regardless of how it is packaged. They don't want to hear anything about the church, since they feel as though the church has sold them a raw deal for centuries. We told them that the rapture was coming during the Millennium causing people to become totally paranoid and defocused on the rights things. Most people that bought into this doctrine were more fixated on the hereafter than they were on the here and now. They thought that to be concerned with anything here and now was carnal, selfish, and ungodly. People gave up on the whole possibility of living life to the max.

People who were in pursuit of their personal destinies gave up everything to begin a totally new path of recruiting people to enlist in the rapture whose final deadline was December 31, 1999. So, many people just became lazy because they thought that Jesus was coming soon. Well, He didn't come back yet, so someone wasn't being honest. The greatest coming of the Lord is by far the revelation of Jesus Christ on the inside of you. When Christ comes to personally visit your life and bring about a total transformation, that is when His light will shine ever so brightly on your inner treasure. Then you will forever know how much you are really worth in the sight of Almighty God. When you discover that, you won't be trying to escape earth, but you will rather want to live forever, knowing that within you live the Spirit of the Living God, who is responsible for every part of your being here.

> *For in him we live, and move, and have our being; as certain also of your own poets have said, For we are also his offspring.*
> *Acts 17:28*

**Believe and Become**

Someone once said, "Man is made by his own belief." As he believes, so is he. Here is a critical question for you. What do you believe? Don't try to give me a theological answer; I'm not concerned with all of that. I don't want you to rehearse something that you've read before. I want you to come from a heart of honesty and conviction. Whatever you really believe is what you will become. Whatever you are saying about yourself is the catalyst for your transformation. Man and woman are both made by his and her belief system. That is why Proverbs 23:7 says, "As a man thinketh so is he." In Matthew 9:29 it says, "According to your faith, be it done unto you."

If you can believe it then you can have it. If you can think it up, then you can think it down. What you believe you will become. This is why you cannot be governed or controlled by your circumstances. Say now, "I am not my circumstances!" Your circumstances will change in life, but your dominant meditative thoughts will always produce what you believe.

*If you can believe it then you can have it. If you can think it up, then you can think it down. What you believe you will become.*

One of the constants in life is growth. From the day you are born into this realm until you exit, you will always be growing. Once you stop growing, death appears. When you stop growing, you stop becoming. A major part of our purpose in life is to continually keep growing until we become formed or shall I say conformed into the image of the Son of God, Jesus the Christ. Allow the image of God to burn within the depths of your soul. "How do I do that?" you ask. You must build yourself up in your most holy faith.

*If you can believe it then you can have it. If you can think it up, then you can think it down. What you believe you will become.*

*But ye, beloved, building up yourselves on your most holy faith, praying in the Holy Ghost. Jude 20*

You must pray in the Spirit, pray from your deepest parts, knowing that you have already received when you pray. That is how you become. You no longer pray asking, or pray begging, but rather you pray knowing that everything is already satisfied in Him. You come to recognize that everything is complete in Him. When you get to this point of true contentment you will realize that nothing outside of yourself really matters. Nothing outside of you can stop you. Opposition is an inescapable fact of life. Everyone who declares a revelatory truth will always have someone or something inject a lie into the orbit, endeavoring to destroy the efficacy of your dream.

Don't buy the lie; believe the truth. Hold fast to your profession. Your profession will become your possession. As citizens of the Kingdom of God you live in a continual state of conquering and living in full dominion of anything outside of you.

> *As it is written, For thy sake we are killed*
> *all the day long; we are accounted as sheep*
> *for the slaughter. Nay, in all these things we*
> *are more than conquerors through him that*

*loved us. For I am persuaded, that neither*
*death, nor life, nor angels, nor principalities,*
*nor powers, nor things present, nor things*
*to come, Nor height, nor depth, nor any*
*other creature, shall be able to separate us*
*from the love of God, which is in Christ*
*Jesus our Lord. Romans 8:36–39*

## Working Your Patience

It is true that faith without works is dead. But there is yet
another thing that you must have in order to perfect your
faith, and that is patience. Without patience you will never
touch the promises of God. There are so many people who
have begun the race of faith, but have faltered less than
halfway into the race because they lacked patience.
Everything that God has promised to you He will perform.
However, you must be patient. You must allow the processes
of God to work itself out in you. It must run its full course.
This is about maturing in God.

*Knowing this, that the trying of your faith*
*worketh patience. But let patience have her*

*perfect work, that ye may be perfect and entire, wanting nothing. James 1:3–4*

Here again we see faith working. This time your faith is working patience whose end result is total abundance. Society is driven by speed. They want to get everything fast and in a hurry. First there were the 286 computers, then the 386 after that, then the Pentium chip, now computers perform at near warp speed and it's going to get even faster. With respect to technology these advancements are absolutely remarkable. With regard to faith though, speed is not a needed factor, waiting is. Remember that your faith is not for God; God doesn't need faith. Your faith is all about revealing you to yourself, and revealing the God in you to yourself. God already knows everything about you. He knows what you are thinking and everything that you are going to do.

You are the one who needs to *"know thyself."* And you will never know what you are going to do in a particular situation, until you are faced with a crisis. When you are faced with a crisis that requires you to stand in faith through it all, your patience will develop the Zoë—God Kind of Character in you. God lasts; and because you are created in His express spiritual similitude, He expects you to last as well. Is there something such as faith without patience? If there is, I will call it a disaster; at best, it is presumption. Biblical faith always requires patience. God has never been impressed with sprinters, as they tend to use up all of their available breath just to run a short distance. God loves endurers, marathoners, those who will endure until the end. The mature finishes their course.

*...you will never know what you are going to do in a particular situation, until you are faced with a crisis.*

# Chapter Three

# Power Keys
# For Liberation Part 1

*You can't separate peace from freedom because no one can be at peace unless he has his freedom.*
*—Malcolm X (1925–1965)*
*Malcolm X Speaks, 1965*

*If the Son therefore shall make you free, ye shall be free indeed. John 8:36*

Liberation should be the goal of every believer in the universe. The whole reason why Jesus came was to bring about liberation to an enslaved people. The strange thing is that most people, who are bound, don't even realize that they are bound until they are far-gone. My prayer is that as you read each of the keys presented here, that you will take an introspective look at yourself and observe whether or not you need improvement in that area. There is nothing in the world like freedom. Freedom is more important than money. In fact, many people purchase their freedom with money.

*Freedom is more*

*important than money.*

The freedom that they were purchasing was more important than the money itself. Our ancestors have taught us a very valuable lesson, and that is this—freedom is not free. There is a price to pay to become free. And yes, freedom is all about becoming. I have carefully prepared a list of power keys with the express intent on helping you to embrace liberation. Each of these keys will unleash in you a new level of freedom and expression. You will know that you have been with God. No longer will you be bound, but for the first time the shackles of religiosity and mental subjugation will not hold you back. So, if you are really serious about apprehending your dream, I have some power keys for you. Now let's begin.

## Power Key # 1
### You must push yourself to the front.

Contrary to popular religious teachings, God is waiting on you to thrust yourself forward and not wait for anyone in life to do it for you. Some things in life you cannot wait for others to do. You've got to do it yourself. I know that there is a false kind of humility going around that suggests that you be really quiet, and that you don't promote yourself. They'll say, "Wait for others to speak well of you. Allow others to promote you. Don't do it yourself. That is conceit, arrogance, and pride to do so." Nothing could be as untrue as that empty statement.

Those are the words of the oppressor who seeks to maim you, and make you feel unworthy before God. If you don't push yourself, who will? You may be waiting for an entire lifetime for someone to understand and ascertain your value in life. You don't have that long to wait. Waiting too long can actually be counterproductive to your destiny. Understand that there is definitely a time to wait, and then there is a time to refrain from waiting and take action. The Holy Spirit within you will inform you of when you should be still from when you should launch out into the deep.

No one in the world will be a more enthusiastic, passionate, and genuine promoter of you, than you. Again, you cannot wait forever to do it. There are times and seasons in life. And the vision that God has conceived on the inside of you, will come forth in its season. However, you will have to push until the baby finally comes out. Do you remember the man who was at the pool of Bethesda? This man could not push himself, or so he thought in his mind. He could not move himself anywhere.

He was so embittered and bound by disappointment that he had become accustomed to waiting. Again, waiting is not a negative thing, but there is a time for everything under the sun. When it comes to seizing divine opportunity in life, you cannot wait around and not take action. You must take action immediately. God knows all things. But God wants to reveal to you whether or not you actually want the things in life that you claim to desire so badly. If you want the best that he has to offer then you will do whatever it takes, even if it means that you have to push yourself.

So many people are waiting for God to do something for them. But in all actuality God is not going to do anything more than He has already done. He has already done enough. Now he is waiting for you to make the move and do something uncommon to get uncommon results. What have you done in the last 30 days that is totally uncommon, totally out of your character? How have you promoted and showcased the God in you in the past week or so.

*God is not going to do anything more than He has already done. He has already done enough. Now he is waiting for you to make the move and do something uncommon.*

Jesus said, "If I be lifted up, I'll draw." The only way to draw men unto you is to lift yourself up, and be seen by those whom God has called you to. "No longer can you be the "best kept secret," saith the Lord. It is time to take your position and be noticed! This man who was by the pool had not pushed himself in 38 years. He acquiesced to just living a lifestyle of being crippled.

> *Now there is at Jerusalem by the sheep market a pool, which is called in the Hebrew tongue Bethesda, having five porches. In these lay a great multitude of impotent folk, of blind, halt, withered, waiting for the moving of the water. For an angel went down at a certain season into the pool, and troubled the water: whosoever then first after the troubling of the water stepped in was made whole of whatsoever disease he had. John 5:2–4*

> *When Jesus saw him lie, and knew that he had been now a long time in that case, he saith unto him, Wilt thou be made whole? John 5:6*

One of the main reasons why people never move forward in the things of God is because they seemingly have a million excuses for why they cannot move forward. This man told the Master many excuses for why he would not embrace his healing, none of which satisfied the Savior. The point here is that Jesus was really trying to get the man to see and understand that his sickness was not really sickness at all, but rather his unwillingness to make a move, different than the ones that he made for thirty-eight years. He exhausted all of his most common excuses.

Jesus asked this man a simple question, one that would end the crisis in his mind about whether or not it was really God's will to heal him. Many people know that it is God's will to heal. Few however, actually believe that God would choose them as primary candidates. Jesus put all of the responsibility of his healing on and in him. That is the only place where healing lives anyway, on the inside of you.

*Healing doesn't come from without, but rather from within.*

Healing doesn't come from without, but rather from within. This man wanted to blame others for why he would not push himself. In the final analysis, it was his primary responsibility to push himself forward. Promoting yourself is not bad. Promoting yourself is God. If you leave that mighty task up to anyone other than yourself, you will not get the job done.

***Power Key # 2***

***Once a man or woman decides on a given course, they become invincible.***

Rev. Ike once said, "There is nothing in life more powerful than a made up mind, because a made up mind is the power of God." I believe that with all of my heart. It doesn't matter whether you are Christian, Jewish, Muslim, Hindi, or Confucian. Once you determine to do something, no force in heaven or earth can stop you. The strange thing is that even if a person decides on doing something wrong, they will still accomplish their mission. A made up mind is extremely powerful.

The older saints in the church would sing a song, "I have decided to follow Jesus, no turning back, no turning back." Sixty and seventy years later, those same saints are still singing the same song. They are still following Jesus. They can't turn back even if they consciously feel like giving up. Their subconscious mind has been trained to keep on following God no matter what. It's much like a good soldier who is trained to fight until the end. Once that decision is made, that is exactly what is going to happen. It works in every area of life.

If you want to be a millionaire within the next six months, make up your mind and decide to become that. Whatever you decide on, you will see happen in your life. Do you want to own a prosperous business, live in the home of your dreams, marry the most charming and beautiful man or woman in the world, have children, or be able to give millions of dollars to children in need? No matter what it is that you want to do, all you have to do is simply decide and you will begin to see the manifestation of your choice materialize.

You ask, "If it is so easy, then why aren't more people actualizing their most expansive dreams? The reason is because many people dream in life, and dreaming is good. But rarely do people decide. I command you in the Name of the Lord, to rise up, wake up, and decide. Deciding today will ultimately pave your tomorrow with better roads. There is mysterious power that clothes the person who makes a decision.

## Power Key # 3
### Spirit is always waiting to be clothed.

The Spirit has very deep desires. One of those desires is to be clothed. Not only does Spirit want us to clothe Him, but also wants us to give Him a name. Whatever name you give Spirit is the name that it will receive, it shall be. When Adam was in the Garden of Eden, he named every animal. And, whatever he named them, that was the name therein. When he named them he also clothed them with that name. Today, the animals, which he named, wear the name.

> *Now the LORD God had formed out of the ground all the beasts of the field and all the birds of the air. He brought them to the man to see what he would name them; and whatever the man called each living creature, that was its name. So the man gave names to all the livestock, the birds of the air and all the beasts of the field. Genesis 2:19–20 NIV*

Like Adam, you too have the power to name everything in your entire world. Whatever you name your situation in life is exactly what it is going to be. If you say, "This isn't going to be good, or I'm gonna lose a lot of money, or I've already lost a lot of money," those words will become clothed around your spirit. You will start wondering how you wound up in that situation. Truth is, you gave it a name. When so-called negative things begin to happen in your life, on your job, or in your region, call on Spirit to witness the power of graduation.

From now on, start naming your obstacles that which you would prefer them to be. Whatever you name your spirit is what you will clothe that spirit with. What you call your situation is what your situation will answer to. No matter how your situation may appear, call it what you desire it to be. Call your chaos peace. Call sickness divine health. Call poverty unfathomable riches. Call yourself blessed every day of your life. The mature believer knows that we do not call things as they are, but rather as we intend them to be. Life will be for you whatever you name it.

*(As it is written, I have made thee a father of many nations,) before him whom he believed, even God, who quickeneth the dead, and calleth those things which be not as though they were. Romans 4:17*

### Power Key # 4
### *You determine your reality by your words.*

Are you in agreement with the negativity that is around you, or have you created a totally different world with the words from your mouth? Can you see past your present situation into the horizon of a brighter day? If you are being bombarded by circumstances and situations that are contrary to your vision for life, you can change that through the power of your faith-filled words. The only people who live in defeat are those who believe that defeat is their permanent address. If defeat is not your reality then don't live there.

You've only turned down a wrong street. Back up, or go forward. No matter what, just keep on moving. People will always tell you what you should do. There are more than enough people in this world who will give you unwarranted advice for free. When I became a pastor, there were people who were quite adamant about how they thought I should behave and were quite clear about what they thought I should be doing. In the beginning, I sort of thought they were right.

But that didn't last very long. I tried hard to meet everyone's expectations. The problem was that I failed to discover my own expectations. When the light shone on me, my eyes opened. I was able to take the blinders off and realize that I was not living my authentic life. I was living my life, trying to please others. It felt like I was adopting foreign ways. The way that I became free from that whole mindset was to start declaring what I knew I was in Christ, and what I wanted for my life, and ministry.

If there was anyone who was going to declare anything over my life, that person should be me. The person who speaks direction into their lives, utilizes the command of their own words, is powerful. Not long after I began to say what I desire, did I begin to see everyone around me, view me totally different than before. The command that God wanted me to have over those He entrusted in my care would not come until first, I commanded myself.

First I had to see myself and speak to myself as a commander. My words shaped my reality. Your words shape your reality. One of the things that many Christians take a very long time to understand is this: In life no one's opinion about you matters. The only word that really matters, the one that takes the highest place in life, is the one that flows from your mouth. You are who you say you are. You are who God says you are.

### Power Key #5
### People respond to your strength of decision

When people ask you who you are, what do you tell them? Your pronouncement about yourself is the image that they will see of you. You should be able to answer with great boldness, "I'm somebody. I am not just anybody. I am called, appointed, and anointed by God our Father. Now is my time, and now is my season. I am the right person for any task that comes my way. I am living my reality. I enjoy living in this universe." Your confident response will cause others to respond to you in the most favorable way. You must be strong when declaring your posture. Continue on by declaring the Word of the Lord.

*I can do all things through Christ which strengtheneth me. Philippians 4:13*

The Word of God needs to unfold to your understanding. The words of the page are meaningless unless they become life to you. Once God spoke to me and said "Debra, I am come that they might have life, and that they might have it more abundantly. (John 10:10) I didn't say man, things, or circumstances, but that I come." The word Zoë in the Greek embodies this whole concept. Zoë means the God kind of life.

Jesus intended that you and I experience the God kind of life, which brings joy, peace, and everything that, you need. But notice God says that we might have it. That tells us that we have a choice in the matter. We must choose to experience the life of God. We must choose the life of God over depression, stress, and oppression. When you choose to no longer identify with your situation, your situation will be forced to change. You have to say, "That is simply not me."

*When you choose to no longer identify with your situation, your situation will be forced to change.*

After a while, your situation will have to take on a new form because of the strength and commitment to your new decision. Any other image that does not conform with the image that you have in your mind is a false image. It is an idol. And all idols must be torn down. One of the greatest enemies to defeat in life is the enemy of ignorance. There is such a zealous anger, perhaps a righteous indignation that comes over me when I see born-again Christians living a life of defeat and saying, "I can't make it because it's too hard."

*Any other image that does not conform with the*

*image that you have in*

*your mind is a false*

*image. It is an idol. And all*

*idols must be torn down.*

You must tell yourself I am a winner. Say it until you begin acting like the winner you claim to be. Walk with a new strut and confidence knowing that you are invincible. Knowledge is a great thing. But if there is anything that you commit to knowing, be sure that you know your own self. When you know your self you become dangerous—especially to the torchbearers of ignorance.

***Power Key # 6***
***You have to deny yourself the illusion and temporary comfort of excuses, for an excuse is a lie that is self-perpetuating.***

Excuses create obstacles to rob you of your dreams.

According to Webster's dictionary, an obstacle is that which prevents forward movement. In your walk with

God there are no excuses. Jesus has taken all excuses to the cross. All excuses have been hanging on that cross more than 2000 years, just as powerless as they were when they were first nailed there. You must begin to view obstacles differently than you have before. Obstacles are challenges, not hindrances. God does not want you to look at life's challenges and say, "Oh God, I cannot do it. Just forget it."

It's not time to throw in the towel. You must embrace obstacles in order to develop into maturity. Don't run away from your obstacles in life. Obstacles are not necessarily negative. They can be used as a barometer to measure how badly you really desire success in life. One truth that I have come to discover is that you cannot totally avert obstacles in life.

The obstacle that you circumvent now will only find you later in life, perhaps at the most inopportune time. Face your challenges head on and conquer them. That is what you are called and equipped to do. Don't make excuses for why you will not move forward. Excuses only delay your inevitable process. Remember, every time you indulge in an excuse you give your circumstances permission to remain unchanged.

## Power Key # 7

### Excuses are happily married to procrastination

> *Then Pharaoh called for Moses and Aaron, and said, Intreat the LORD, that he may take away the frogs from me, and from my people; and I will let the people go, that they may do sacrifice unto the LORD. And Moses said unto Pharaoh, Glory over me: when shall I intreat for thee, and for thy servants, and for thy people, to destroy the frogs from thee and thy houses, that they may remain in the river only? And he said, To morrow. And he said, Be it according to thy word: that thou mayest know that there is none like unto the LORD our God. Exodus 8:8–10*

Here we see that Moses went to Pharaoh and asked, "When do you want the frogs to leave?" Pharaoh answered, "Tomorrow." It's quite obvious that there was no real urgency in Pharaoh's life. It's quite apparent that the Pharaoh had become very comfortable with his situation.

You can be in a situation so long, even if it's a negative one that you begin to acclimate to it. Once you begin to become accustomed to a not-so-good situation you will become a master procrastinator at doing anything that will move you from that situation.

Perhaps after so many plagues, he started to enjoy the drama of the plagues. Obviously he didn't mind seeing the frogs in his house, and in his pool, in his bed, and in his drinking water. Why didn't he tell Moses to pray to God and get rid of the frogs immediately? Like many believers today, Pharaoh allowed himself to have a long-term affair with procrastination.

He kissed procrastination so long that he became the thing (procrastination) that he beheld. Don't put off for tomorrow that which you must do today. Procrastination is the enemy to your progress and spiritual development. If God moves upon your soul to fast and pray, don't put it off until later. God is trying to work something out inside of you, right now. Your failure to execute the task, and take action, only prolongs the process and puts on hold the manifold riches that God has in store for you.

***Power Key # 8, When you are truly tired of your messy situation, you will stop talking about change, and you will make a decision to just act.***

When you really want change in your life it won't happen tomorrow, next week, or next year it will happen now. There was a song that we used to sing in church that had a line saying, "I'm gonna wait until my change comes." I think that somehow many Christians have become engulfed by the message of that gospel song, allowing it to paralyze them.

You are not supposed to wait until your change comes. You are supposed to demand your change to come by taking right-now action. The Bible says: Now faith is the substance of things hoped for, the evidence of things not seen. Hebrews 11:1. There is no need to sit idly by just waiting for something to happen in life for you. You must initiate change in life. Do something!

***Power Key # 9, Learn and discern the time and the people that are in your life.***

You must always evaluate the people who are in your life, as they are a direct reflection of you. In the same way that you may do a major cleaning in your house every spring, you must also do a spring-cleaning in your own life, getting rid of anything, any place, or any person that is not conducive for your growth. Abraham could not travel to where he was going with his nephew Lot. They had to part. There are times when you are just not going to be able to go to the next level with the people you are hanging with.

*Any other image that does not conform with the image that you have in your mind is a false image. It is an idol. And all idols must be torn down.*

I know this area can be one of great sensitivity, especially since the people, who are in your life, may have been there a long time, and you've gotten accustomed to them. But God is saying that it is time to get rid of those Lots in your life, because they are stopping your progress. You argue, "They are family, or I've been knowing him or her for twenty years. Lord, I've known her for more than 20 years.

Lord, I have been at this church for 15 years, and you haven't called me to leave this place. My mother and grandmother went there too." Get rid of the Lot! It doesn't matter how you phrase it, there is not enough room for you and someone else whose vision, purpose, and values are in diametric opposition to yours.

*Can two walk together, except they be agreed? Amos 3:3*

It is clear here that two cannot walk together unless they are in agreement. Many people have much more than one other person in their life, preventing them from moving forward. Unfortunately, people who are not moving forward in life, often have an entire army of people who are holding them back. But the bottom line is that no one can hold you back without your express permission. You let people hold you back.

There is a parcel of land that God wants to give you that is green and fresh. There's a fresher walk that God wants you to walk, but as long as you have some Lots—distractions, hindrances, and plain nuisances in your life, you will never reach the place in God or the place in life that God intended for you. Abraham and Lot worked together until they outgrew each other. Genesis 13:6 says, "And the land was not able to bear them, that they might dwell together: for their substance was great, so that they could not dwell together."

*There are people that you*
*will outgrow in life.*
*When that happens, you have*
*to move on. Don't stay there.*
*If you try to stay there, then*
*you too will become as them,*
*depreciating in value.*

There are people that you will outgrow in life. When that happens, you have to move on. Don't stay there. If you try to stay there, then you too will become as them, depreciating in value. This isn't about status. This is about the value of the mind. The way that you grow in life is by growing your mind, and opening up your mind to new ideas and fresh opportunities. People that want you to stay in the same place that you've always been with them are selfish.

A true friend, a faithful family member will always want you to move forward in life, even if that means that you may have to surpass them on the way. The relationship that Abraham shared with Lot was at one time very prosperous and mutually beneficial. However, this once good union went sour because somebody stopped growing. When that happens in life, somebody has to go. Somebody has to go in order for you to grow. The longer that you stay around them, the quicker you will suffocate from a mind that lacks proper air.

So, how do you discern a Lot in your life? A Lot is anyone that is not adding to you. If someone is making consistent withdrawals from your life and never adding to you, they are a Lot. If they are squeezing the very life out of you, you must get rid of them. I know this word may seem a bit hard. Accept it anyway. This truth will save your life and cause you to enter into your land of promise. Choose to make the change. Change your company and change your outcome, forever!

# Chapter Four
## Power Keys
## For Liberation, Part 2

**Power Key # 10**

**_Making changes involve a measure of risk._**

> _It seems to me that people have vast potential._
> _Most people can do extraordinary things if_
> _they have the confidence or take the risks._
> _Yet most people don't. They sit in front of_
> _the telly and treat life as if it goes on forever._
> _Phillip Adams_

Successful people from every stratum of life and in nearly every discipline all have one thing in common. Successful people often take risks. They make friends with the threat of failure. They never hide from the possibility of potential defeat, knowing that passing through this rite of passage is the only way to enter into their land of promise. Fear paralyzes you, causing you to become comfortable in a state of inertia. There is not one person in the spiritual world who enjoys success who has not taken major risks in their ministry or movement to become successful.

*Successful people*

*often take risks.*

I cannot stress this point enough. Our society tends to steer people away from risk taking. We see this all of the time. Investment gurus may tell you not to invest in a stock since it has a high risk factor. They will in turn advice you to invest in a low load mutual fund that yields a far less return over a very long period of time. "Don't worry though, it's safe," they'll say. There are so many people who have never purchased a home because they were just waiting for the right time to buy. They were afraid to take the risk in the seventies, and eighties.

They did not want to lose. Now thirty years later, they still haven't capitalized on the many opportunities that have come and gone since then. They were afraid to take the risk and now have missed out on the greater joys that life has to offer. The truth is that the people who encourage you to never take risks are benefiting in a big way from your safety. In a recent Forbes article, an apartment building magnate expressed his extreme happiness because of the declining housing market. He does not care if the market never goes back up.

He does not want the people to take the risk to buy a home. Why is that? He is making a major profit from renters staying in the safety zone. In life you should gravitate toward the people who provoke you to take risks, not those who don't. The only way that you will ever become successful is to get out of your place of certainty and begin to dwell in the place of uncertainty—the place where God lives. Colonel Sanders the founder and brander of the world famous Kentucky Fried Chicken, now known as KFC ™, was nearing retirement when he made the quality decision that he did not want to depend on social security.

He began to visualize a life far beyond the low level that he had accepted for too long. Sanders looked at what he had to offer and saw great value in his secret fried chicken recipe, a recipe that had been in his family for generations. He could have wallowed in the bleakness of his circumstances, and cried about how little he had to show for a lifetime of hard work, working multiple menial jobs. Instead he saw precious gold within himself and began to mine the fields and discovered Kentucky Fried Chicken. Was it a major risk for this senior citizen? Absolutely yes!

But you have to come to the place in your life where you have already lost so much that you really don't have anything else to lose. That is when your risk taking won't even matter. Now I am not trying to get you to do something reckless. I believe that you should make calculated decisions in life. I am not telling you to risk it all, like you were playing your life away on the craps table. What I am saying is that you will never have any idea what kind of joy is actually possible, until you step out of your safety zone and do something that you never did before.

The whole concept here is that what you are willing to lose will determine the gain you will receive in life. Always stay focused on the benefits of your risk taking. It's the benefits in life that you are going after, so stay focused on them. As soon as you forget the benefits you begin to focus on the negative potential consequences of the risk you have taken. When that happens, you will lose it all. But remember this, the greater the risk, the greater the value of your success.

### Power Key # 11
### There is nothing that is too big for you to conquer.

> *They can conquer who believe they can.*
> *Virgil*

There is nothing in life that you cannot have. First though, you must elevate your mind. Your thoughts have to come up to an entirely higher level. Some concepts you must catch in the spirit. That is the only way you will ever understand them. You may not know initially how to do that; it may take some time. What you do know is that God said it in his Word. And if God said it, then it is so. Our understanding may come later, but the Word is already settled in heaven.

*God is not a man, that he should lie; neither the son of man, that he should repent: hath he said, and shall he not do it? or hath he spoken, and shall he not make it good?*
*Numbers 23:19*

You have to look at every situation in your life and see beyond your present state into the mind of God for your life. Where you are now is not where you will be. You must project your mind into the place where you will be. With God nothing is impossible. All things are possible! "I know you said that I would be in my own business, but I have no idea how that will ever happen, because of the way the economy is going. Things seem so unstable and I don't know how God will actually pull this one off."

One of the main reasons why people do not tap into their God potential is because they micromanage their own situations. Everyone has a part to play. You must allow God full sway in your life to do what He does best. One of the most dangerous and totally unproductive things that you could ever do is to sit around trying to figure out how God does what He does. If God gave you that information then you would become God in personality rather than being god in principle.

Throughout my life, I can honestly say that God has brought me through some things, that even until this day, I have no idea how He did it. What He did was absolutely amazing. Now I don't even bother trying to figure out the "how." Instead, I just give thanks. That's all. That's how I simplify my life and increase the favor on my life.

> *And Jesus looking upon them saith, With*
> *men it is impossible, but not with God:*
> *for with God all things are possible.*
> *Mark 10:27*

All things are possible with God. "All things" means just that—ALL THINGS. It is time for the people of God to once and for all eradicate any thoughts that try to exalt itself against the knowledge of God. When Jesus said that with God all things are possible, He was trying to get them to understand that God defies all realms of human logic and reasoning.

*God is guaranteeing you*
*success by simply believing*
*and acting in His Word.*

The things that God does, do not, and will not make sense to the average person in society. His ways causes the wise to feel foolish. God takes away all excuses from you not wanting to do big things in life. In short, God is guaranteeing you success by simply believing and acting in His Word. Your job is to simply believe. God's job is to perform the task.

### Power Key # 12
### Don't be afraid to reach for Greatness

*If you would attain greatness, think no little thoughts.—Anonymous*

Greatness always exists in the area of the unknown. Don't be afraid of the unknown. Most people are scared to death of the unknown and tend to shy away from anything that appears to threaten their sense of security. At times, you will have to release everything that you have held so dear in life just to you can step into your future. Let go and let God! Do this especially when God requires you to step out into your purpose.

One of life's greatest fears is the fear of failure. So many people choose to do nothing, or at best live average lives, because they are afraid of failing. Honestly speaking, if you haven't stepped into your purpose, you have already signed an agreement with failure. God is waiting for you to step up. Even if you did fail, you still have God on your side, which means everything in the world. If you fall, He is right there to catch you, pick you back up, and set you back on the pathway to success.

Mature believers are not afraid of failing. However, they are concerned about failing God. You fail God when you do not take Him at His Word. You fail God when you are too afraid to be great, since no one in your family was great. God's expecting greatness from you. Don't dishearten Him.

*Mature believers are not afraid of failing. However, they are concerned about failing God. You fail God when you do not take Him at His Word.*

*Now the LORD had said unto Abram, Get thee out of thy country, and from thy kindred, and from thy father's house, unto a land that I will shew thee: And I will make of thee a great nation, and I will bless thee, and make thy name great; and thou shalt be a blessing: And I will bless them that bless thee, and curse him that curseth thee: and in thee shall all families of the earth be blessed. Genesis 12:1–3*

Here we see that God made a promise to Abram to make his name great. What you must realize is that God could have never made Abram great or made his name great without Abram's permission and his personal involvement. God doesn't just make anybody anything. You must be ready for greatness. Being great must be in your heart. It must be in your consciousness. If you do not want greatness because you are afraid of what others might think of you, then you won't qualify.

*One of the main reasons*
*why people are timid*
*about greatness is because*
*they are too concerned*
*about what their familiar*
*circle of friends and family*
*may say about them.*

One of the main reasons why people are timid about greatness is because they are too concerned about what their familiar circle of friends and family may say about them. I believe that this same thing may have gone through Abram's mind, wondering what people might say. Abram knew that he would perhaps have to deal with his family. When you become great, people always want you to make an excuse for your greatness. They want you to have a reason to justify why you have become great without their consent. You have to make a formal apology for your success. This is not God.

In truth, you don't owe anyone an excuse, apology, or explanation for the blessings of the Lord over your life. You don't have to explain the blessings and favor of God on your life to anyone. God only requires that you just walk in it. Interestingly, God gives Abram some specific instructions, which I believe is the measuring stick that will determine whether or not a person is eligible to receive His greatness. In life there is always a price to pay for anything of value.

*If you are a person who cannot release your family and just leave, in order to receive God's best, then you will never be great.*

The basest introductory test is the family test. If you are a person who cannot release your family and just leave, in order to receive God's best, then you will never be great. This is not coming against family. Family is wonderful, but there are times when family can block the flow of favor in your life. When that happens, you have to make a decision. Do I continue to deal with people who are holding me back, or do I break free from the bonds of familial ties and just be great? I think you already know the right answer. Since you know, just do it!

*And every one that hath forsaken houses, or brethren, or sisters, or father, or mother, or wife, or children, or lands, for my name's sake , shall receive an hundredfold, and shall inherit everlasting life. Matthew 19:29*

## Power Key # 13
## Faith Never Says No

*Then touched he their eyes, saying, According to your faith be it unto you. Matthew 9:29*

By faith, you need to arise in the power and strength of the Lord and get what is rightfully yours. If you can believe it they you can have it. If you can think it then you will touch it. Trust in God's infinite supply. Knowing that there is no end in infinity, no end in God, you can be certain that your faith will always reward you with whatever your heart desires. This is not like applying for a home mortgage, where you may be turned down if you do not fit the profile that the lender desires.

There are times when a certain lender can only lend out a certain amount of money in any given quarter. Once they have reached that cap, they have to wait for another season to replenish their money. Not so with God, God never runs out of supply. So whatever you need from Him is always present. The way that you access His supply is by using your faith. Consider faith as your private escort into the realms of possibilities. Faith will reward you whatever you are big enough to believe for. However, you must change your perspective on what you believe is big.

Through your eyes, which are God's eyes, you cannot really see anything as being too big. Big things will start to look just as normal as ever, because you don't see anything thing as small. In order to view things this way, you have to have a different kind of spirit. When everybody goes one way, you have to maintain your ground and go the other way. You are not like everybody else. You do not think like the group. God has called you out, to be an out-of-the-box thinker.

> *But my servant Caleb, because he had another spirit with him, and hath followed me fully, him will I bring into the land whereinto he went; and his seed shall possess it. Number 14:24*

Caleb had another spirit, and because of that God favored him. He was able to do things and go places that the children of Israel were not. When you allow your faith to become your guide and the way you live your everyday life, you will begin to have access into places that only the select few has entered.

> *And the LORD spake unto Moses, saying, Send thou men, that they may search the land of Canaan, which I give unto the children of Israel: of every tribe of their fathers shall ye send a man, every one a ruler among them. Numbers 13:1–2*

> *And Caleb stilled the people before Moses, and said, Let us go up at once, and possess it; for we are well able to overcome it. Numbers 13:30*

God, through Moses, told the people to go and search out the land. When Caleb returned from the land, his report was "Let us go up and possess it, for we are well able to overcome it." The average person would have used every possible excuse not to go back into the land. But here Caleb is speaking with bold confidence about their ability to conquer the land.

> *And they told him, and said, We came unto the land whither thou sentest us, and surely it floweth with milk and honey; and this is the fruit of it. Nevertheless the people be strong that dwell in the land, and the cities are walled, and very great: and moreover we saw the children of Anak there.*
> *Numbers 13:27–28*

The people in this land were giants but that didn't matter to Caleb. What Caleb focused on was the milk and honey and the large fruit in the land. He focused not on his small stature in comparison to the giants of the land, but rather how God graciously gave him jurisdictional authority over the giants. There is a tremendous lesson to learn here.

You, as well as everyone else, will have giants in your life. For some, the giants destroy them. Others allow the giants to enslave them and get them addicted to unhealthy things. The better option is when you get your giants working for your cause in life. It's true that God will really make your enemies your footstool. The very thing that came to destroy you will in turn become your life partner helping you to receive all that good that you desire. It all starts with faith. Then it builds on faith. Finally it ends with faith.

***Power Key # 14***
***Reasoning is the embryo of unbelief and will rob your miracle.***

*In a purely intellectual world, reasoning is the thing that earns you merit. However in God's World, or should I say in the Kingdom of God, too much reasoning will get you in trouble*

In a purely intellectual world, reasoning is the thing that earns you merit. However in God's World, or should I say in the Kingdom of God, too much reasoning will get you in trouble. You will reason God out of the equation. Some things are not left to reason, but only require simple obedience. God is asking, "What giants are you killing? What giant will you destroy for my glory? What victories will you win for me today?

How will you display me in the earth? Where are your mighty acts?" Your response should always be in the affirmative. Never answer God with reason. That only irritates God. When God told Moses to go and tell Pharaoh to "Let my people go," Moses reasoned with God, "I am slow of speech and tongue." He reasoned that he was not eligible because he was not as articulate as he would have liked to have been.

> *And Moses said unto the LORD, O my Lord,*
> *I am not eloquent, neither heretofore, nor*
> *since thou hast spoken unto thy servant: but*
> *I am slow of speech, and of a slow tongue.*
> *And the LORD said unto him, Who hath*
> *made man's mouth ? or who maketh the*

*dumb, or deaf, or the seeing, or the blind?*

*have not I the LORD? Exodus 4:10–11*

God asked, "Who made your mouth Moses?" Moses' reasoning was no good for God. God never needs your reasoning when He asks you to do something. You will reason yourself, (and the people with whom you are connected) out of a miracle. If God accepted Moses' reason as worthy and excused him from delivering the children of Israel, where would we be today as a spiritual people? Your obedience can change the course of history, and set nations afire.

Being married to my prophetic husband, quite often he speaks of things that I cannot behold with my natural eyes. Why is it that I don't always see what he sees? I don't see it because my womanhood will speak from my need for security. As a mother, I am often motivated by family concerns. That is my reasoning. When I go into my secret place, the Father will say to me, "Debra, didn't I say I would lead thee and guide thee with Mine own eyes? Didn't I tell you that you can believe Me and what I will do? Just trust me."

When I began to rest on God's Word to me, His peace followed. Now, I totally release the need to have to understand everything that my husband sees in the Spirit. My position is to continue to put my trust in the Lord. Everything else will work out just fine. Train yourself to begin viewing things through the eyes of the spirit.

### Power Key # 15
### Stop demeaning yourself

Nothing is worse than a person who continually degrades himself or herself. Believe me when I tell you that you will have more than enough people in life to do that. You surely don't have to help them. One of the reasons why many believers, especially those who have just begun the walk with Christ, have developed such a poor image about themselves is because of the doctrine they've been taught. Many fundamental believers espouse a teaching of unworthiness.

Perhaps you have heard people crying out to God and praying aloud shouting, "Lord, I am so unworthy. I am nothing in your eyes, oh God. I am like dung. I am a dog. I am worthless." That kind of talk has been accepted in church circles for centuries. I have to let you know that God has never accepted any of that. In fact, that kind of stuff doesn't please God at all, but rather disappoints Him. If you were unworthy, then that would mean that Christ's substitutionary sacrifice was worthless.

This would mean that Jesus would have to die all over again, because the first death was not strong enough to make you and me worthy. You are worthy! This is not because you did something so important. You are worthy because of the blood that Jesus shed. Jesus paid the price to make you worthy. So if you ever run around crying about how unworthy you are, you are making Jesus out to be a liar. God made no mistakes when he made you.

Everything about you is very intentional. You are not a mistake, but rather you are a part of God's ultimate plan to make this earth a better place. He didn't just throw you together by accident. Like a master craftsman, God created you and fashioned you after His likeness. To think any other way, is tantamount to taking the Lord's name and His sacrifice in vain. Never demean that which God has made.

*I will praise thee; for I am fearfully and wonderfully made: marvellous are thy works; and that my soul knoweth right well. Psalms 139:14*

### Power Key # 16
### *You will become whatever rents space in your mind*

We are not creatures of circumstances. We are creators of our divine reality. There is a difference. A creature waits for others to give it permission to apprehend, while a creator dictates and exercises his divine right of choice. Creators know where they are going in life. They decree a thing and the thing decreed becomes so. Creatures wallow in wishes, usually the wishes of others. Since we are made in God's image we have the innate ability to create.

*We are not creatures of circumstances. We are creators of our divine reality.*

It is your God ordained right to create. Your mind is a repository for anything that you feed it. The entire Bible is about getting you to become like God, think like God, and look like God. You have forgotten your original position. God made you to have dominion over the earth and rule like He rules. If that remained the dominate thought in your mind throughout the course of your life, your entire life would be drastically different.

Instead we've allowed other people's words, to control the way we think. Unfortunately many of us have allowed those self defeating thoughts to park in our mind, leaving us with no other choice than to become the thing that dwells in the mind. The most important thing that you can ever meditate on is the fact that you are the express image of God. You are God's representative in the earth. You are God's spokesperson on earth. When you speak it is the voice of God speaking for you create with the words of your mouth. You are co-creator with God.

# *It is your God ordained right to create.*

**Power Key # 17 Nothing comes to those who do not believe in their divinity.**

> *Shew the things that are to come hereafter, that we may know that [ye are gods]: yea, do good, or do evil, that we may be dismayed, and behold it together. Isaiah 41:23 (brackets author's own)*

If you don't believe in you God-self, if you don't believe that God has called you, that he has ordained you, and that the very same power that we read about in the Bible eternally resides on the inside of you, you will be ineffective in life. When I was a child I used to always imagine, "Oh, if only I could have lived during the Bible days." I've stopped saying that.

I have learned to appreciate and embrace the day and time in which I now live. God allowed me to live in this time because He knew the role that I would play out in life required me to be here now, and not back then. These are the good days, right here and now. Everyday that you wake up in your right mind you must declare, "Lord, this is the day that you have made. I am going to rejoice therein Father." "What can I do to make you happy today? How can I satisfy you?"

By taking this approach to every thing in life, you will be in the driver's seat at all times. The whole concept of the enemy is really a farce. The only enemy that exists is the one that you have given place to in your mind. When you take your rightful stance in life, and declare to the universe your oneness with God, any opposing force will have to halt its move before launching an attack. You see no one wants to fight with God, for everyone recognizes that to fight God and expect to win would be next to impossible.

So when you are properly grounded, everyone knows that you cannot be easily shaken. It is not so much that you have to announce to the world who you are, although there is a time and season for that too. But the God authority that you are draped with should be a sign to anyone wishing to engage in battle with you, to think twice before engaging. It is for you to know this. You must be very aware of your god-self. Your flesh can be easily destroyed. Your god-self cannot be destroyed because it is spirit.

*Your god-self cannot*
*be destroyed because*
*it is spirit.*

In you dwells the same power of Jesus Christ, and the same power of the Apostles. The Greater One lives on the inside of you so you really are invincible. There is nothing that God cannot do through you, if only you will allow Him the chance.

*Ye are of God, little children, and have overcome them: because greater is he that is in you, than he that is in the world.*

*1 John 4:4*

## Chapter Five
# Life Is Waiting For You

A story was once told about a young man who desired to come to America. For years he labored and struggled until he finally saved enough money to purchase the ticket for the next ship sailing to the New World. After paying for his board, he did not know whether or not he would have enough money to buy food. So he decided to stay in the cabin the entire trip, nibbling on a few crackers that he brought with him, hoping that it would sustain him for the long journey, while he was forced to live in deprivation.

This man would not partake of anything that this great cruise ship had to offer for he believed that he would have to pay for it, and he just didn't have the money. What he did not recognize was that his fare to the New World also included food on this beautiful ship three times daily, plus all of the snacks desired. There were parties, and several other social functions going on, all included in his fare, yet not knowing, he stayed away and nearly starved to death. This man missed out on all of these great benefits because he was unaware. What is it that you are unaware of?

Many people sail through life with that self same attitude as this hopeful man had, living deprived, because they haven't yet realized the benefits of life. There are people who choose not to actively participate because they do not realize that Christ has allowed them to come to this world so they can become anything they desire to be. Life is all about fulfillment.

You can fulfill your life's purpose and lead a life of rich meaning and contribution. It is about time that you come into the perfect knowledge that God did not put you on earth to live a lifestyle of drudgery and defeat. Far from that, God wants you to enjoy life. He wants you to have plenty of fun. And yes, you can have a wonderful time while you are actively engaging in the work of the Lord.

The church has actively participated in helping you to feel pitiful about your self. The church by and large has perpetuated a false doctrine that makes people feel as though God wants them to barely make it, to have just enough to get by, and to avoid any semblance of prosperity and financial riches, as it would cause one to become tainted and unholy. That is what the church has taught its hundreds of millions of followers for centuries.

Today, we have a handful of ministries who teach that God wants His people to prosper and be in health. However, those ministries are dwindling down to barely anything as social and political pressure comes bearing down on them. Some of them still teach the message, but few actually demonstrate it, in fear of being judged. The whole idea of you enjoying life is a God idea, not mans. Leaders need to begin boldly teaching its followers that your enjoyment in life is a high priority in the heart of God.

Since so many spiritual leaders have taught just the opposite, and have taught it so long, the average person in society views the lifestyle of churchgoers as tedious and uninteresting. The church has plenty of people who are crying out for attention as they suffer through this life for the cause of Christ. The problem with this picture of false humility is that Christ never ordered for them to suffer in this way.

Much of the pain that we bear in the Name of Christ is self-inflicted pain, much like the self-flagellations bore by extreme followers of Opus Dei and other similar factions. God is waiting on you to catch this revelation. You were not put on this earth to be subjected to a never-ending cycle of pain and defeat. If that were the case, your life would be most miserable. No, you were put on this earth to give to the earth. That which you give unto the earth, will be returned unto you in due season.

*Much of the pain that we bear in the Name of Christ is self-inflicted pain...*

In many cases, much of the pain we suffer can be directly linked to our inability to sow the proper seeds during the right season. Would it be fair for the farmer to cry and complain about why he has not reaped a sufficient harvest even though he did not sow seeds in the previous season?

That would be most absurd. He cannot expect to eat from robust crops if he hadn't planted seeds the season before. So then, the good life that God intends for you to enjoy is actualized by:

1. openly receiving and accepting a life of enjoyment as God's high priority for you.

2. sowing plenty of seeds that will ensure that you will be able to eat the good of the land in any given season.

3. waiting with eager expectation for the harvest to become ripe.

4. reaping the harvest and repeating the cycle all over again.

As simple as these steps are, we often complicate the entire process by allowing outside influences and the opinions of others to weaken our resolve. You cannot be intimidated by what people are dictating to you. For as long as you live, there will always be people who do not see things the way you do in life. There will always be people who will oppose your prosperity. There will be people, few though, who will fight long and hard to get riches into your hands. Those people, you should hold onto for as long as you can, for they are very rare.

People live on both sides of the fence. What you must understand is that they will always be there, on both sides. However, your life has nothing to do with either opinion. The quality of your life must be reflected by God's will for you. Deep within your heart, you must bear the conviction that God wants you to have all the good that you desire. If no one understands that, fine. The one who should be most convinced of this truth is you. There are times when you should buy things that make you happy, regardless of what others may think.

Believe me when I tell you that people will do what they want to do. They will purchase anything they feel fit to. As soon as you buy something that you like, then they get funny and start acting strange. You must get delivered from their attitudes and judgments about you. Start enjoying and loving YOU! Enjoy the Christ that is on the inside of you. Don't come to the end of your life, only to realize that you've only lived a mere fragment.

God wants you to live in the overflow. As you mature in Him you will come to know this. You will realize that a life of pleasing others is not necessarily a life that pleases God. God is an extremist. He is an extravagant God. Just look around in the universe and you will behold the beauty and enormity of His awesome creation. Slave religion has done a marvelous job of convincing you that it is not God's will for you to have the best, while the oppressor glibly swayed you into believing that you should eat his scraps. He told you that this would please the Lord.

*Slave religion has done a marvelous job of convincing you that it is not God's will for you to have the best...*

This is why more teaching is needed with regard to the mind, and the mind of God in you. When you know within that you are God's progeny you will act like children of the king, not subjects of the slave master. Traditional religion, again, has done a remarkable job in enslaving the minds of believers and convincing them that they are not supposed to enjoy life, have wealth, or to think objectively and critically. "We will think for you," is their creed. The Word of God clarifies this whole area.

> *Now unto him that is able to do exceeding abundantly above all that we ask or think, according to the power that worketh in us.*
> *Ephesians 3:20*

God's power works on the inside of YOU! God can only do exceedingly and abundantly in your life if you are able to think. That is something that many people have failed to realize. If you are not a thinker, that will limit God's ability to do great things for you. You have to think of how you desire your life to be in another month, year, or five years from now. Use your mind to visualize the kind of contribution you desire to make in the world. What kinds of impact do you want to leave on society? Where have you always dreamed of traveling? Where do you want to live?

What kind of revenue do you really see your business earning annually? What about your own income, wouldn't it be great for that to double, too? Where do you envision your children going to college? Who will they marry? You see, all of these questions, and many more that you can add to this list, all require thought. If you do not think then you will tie God's hands and limit His effectiveness. That is the main reason why people do not enjoy life.

*Stop placing limitations on yourself that organized religion and public opinion has set forth. In God there is no limits.*

You must employ the Laws of Thinking. One of the finest primers on this subject is New York Times Bestseller, *The Laws of Thinking: 20 Secrets to Using the Divine Power of Your Mind To Manifest Prosperity,* by my husband, Bishop E. Bernard Jordan. You will think your way into a better life, and his remarkable work will show you how to do just that. But you must first believe that you deserve better than what you have right now.

You cannot be moved by your financial position right now. You must know in your heart of hearts that where you are right now is no indication of where you will be on tomorrow. Stop placing limitations, on yourself, that organized religion and public opinion has set forth. In God there is no limits. And because He resides within, you have no limits either.

## Take The Limits Off

Whether you are young or old, do not allow anyone to set limitations on your life. I've heard people in general give advice to the older people to slow down and take it easy in life. They're told to settle down and relax because they are getting too old to keeping moving at a fast pace. Take those limits that other people have placed on you, and keep moving forward. In fact, you should go even faster than you did before. Do not allow people to erect thick walls of limitation in your thinking.

The church is full of people who have allowed the enemy of their minds, and unfruitful thoughts to limit their progress in life. Become a master of ignoring all of the negative and limiting things that people have to say about your race, creed, age, or even beliefs. Take the limits off! A few years ago, I told my husband when I turn 40 I might just do something drastic, something really unexpected. "Maybe I may cut all my hair off, or I might just get braids all the way down past my waist." Am I saying this to garner the attention of people? No, absolutely not!

This is about me. I am going to enjoy a new experience because I will be walking in a new dimension. When you move into a new level of life, it should be seen outwardly. Not everybody knows what's going on inside of you. But what's going on inside should be reflected outside. The message that you are projecting, or at least the one I wanted to project, was that I am taking the limits off. I am taking the limits off that the church at large had placed on me. I am taking the limits off that my children placed on me. I am taking the limits that society placed on me.

There is this view of what a woman out to be like in society, take the limits off and live beyond and above their expectations. There is an image of what a pastor's wife ought to look like. Recreate a totally new image that is conducive with your personality and the way God made you to be. Stop trying to fit into other people's modes. You will come to the end of your life miserable, frustrated, and unfulfilled.

When you do something totally different, people may believe that you are going through a mid-life crisis. Don't worry about that. In actuality, you are really breaking free from the crisis of public opinion. I am walking through life knowing that I have a one-way ticket through this frame of reality, and I am determined to enjoy the ride as long as it lasts.

You too, need to embrace this same reality. Enjoy life! Laugh! Experience life in new ways. Being reared in a very strict ascetic religious background, my impression of being a good Christian, especially as a young woman was, wearing a long dress, long sleeves, and prayer caps to cover my head. I discovered in the midst of all of that, I could still live a holy lifestyle and have an incredible time enjoying life simultaneously. I didn't have to choose one or the other.

God has no problem with me going out to have a fine dinner with my husband. I can go out and dance with my husband and still bear witness to the Lordship of Jesus

Christ. In fact, what better place is there to be a witness to a people in need of Christ's hope? A two-timing lover has burned someone on that dance floor. And they are using the dance floor to vent and release off some steam. They're angry with their partner, angry with themselves, and angry with God. Thank God though; they are not angry with me.

Because I am not judging them, I can easily approach them in any environment, because I am a believer. I don't mind going to where they are, and lifting them up. All believers are called to go beyond living God's Word to becoming His Word. The latter only happens when you choose to become mature and perfected. That happens when you begin to take the limits off.

*All believers are called to go beyond living God's Word to becoming His Word.*

## Living Epistles

When people read you are they reading the Word of God, or a sad story? We are to be living epistles so that men and women everywhere can see the expression of God's Love in us and through us. Don't be afraid to share your life's experiences with others, especially those that you did not believe you'd make it through. It is those kinds of transparent moments that encourage other fellow travelers to have hope, once again, in God.

Tell them, "Look upon me. This is what God did. This is what God can do. If He did it for me, surely He will do the same for you." You can have a testimony service wherever you are; don't wait until you go to church. You cannot make an impact on others without making contact with others. You have to touch the people where they are.

> *But when he saw the multitudes, he was moved with compassion on them, because they fainted, and were scattered abroad, as sheep having no shepherd. Matthew 9:36*

*It doesn't matter how many mistakes you made. Mistakes can be used as stepping-stones to propel you to the place where you need to go.*

Jesus touched the people where they were. He was moved with compassion. We must be moved in the same manner as Christ was. Don't isolate yourself from the very people you are called to touch. Jesus showed himself to the people from various walks of life. He didn't discriminate against anyone, so why should we?

It doesn't matter how many mistakes you made. Mistakes can be used as stepping-stones to propel you to the place where you need to go. So what if you made a mistake, or even a great big one. So what if you weren't as effective as you thought you should have been. As long as there is life and breath in your body, there is always the next time.

## Failure Comes Before Perfection

Imagine how different our lives would be today, if the Wright brothers, Wilbur and Orville, allowed their many failures to stop them from pursuing their dreams of air flight. Today we would not have an aviation industry. Life would be much slower. Things that are needed quickly such as emergency medication for the sick, and food for people who have experienced a tragedy such as the tsunami in Sri Lanka would all have to be put on hold.

Without air flight, it would take months or even up to a year or more to get emergency services to the people. In that time, millions could die. The good thing is that these Wright brothers didn't give up. Their own father was not supportive of their idea, and thought that it was just some "pie in the sky" concept that would never happen. That didn't stop them either. They determined to become perfected. Some of the most amazing inventions ever made, came as a result of multiple failures before they ever became available to the masses.

A true inventor understands that failure is a necessary process to growth and development. Each failure becomes one of many volumes of chapters of what not to do. The "what not to do" in life can be just as important as "what to do." Knowing what not to do will cause you to grow faster, and to perform with much more accuracy as you will not have to continually repeat failed patterns. The successful in life do not see failure as their inquisitor, taking them to trial to pass a negative judgment or punishment upon them.

Successful people never give up, and neither should you. Your past is the worse indicator of your future. Your passion dictates your future. In the final analysis of things, there really are no failures in life. The universe perceives no failure. We are all overcomers through Jesus Christ. Stop consulting your past, for it cannot prophesy into your future. The past is merely an illusion. It came to past. It was here, and now, it is no longer. The only thing that is of vital importance is the nowness of God.

# *Your passion dictates your future.*

What you decide right now will determine what you are going to do in the future. It's "now" faith that gets results, not next year faith. Make up your mind right now. Make a clear-cut decision to live life to the max. Your decisions will catapult you to your next level in God. Whatever you believe will determine your outcome. Remember that you must begin by making the choice to choose. Yes, you may have opposition.

You may have an inner war going on inside of you. Don't worry about that. Ignore all outside influences. The life that you are getting ready to enter into is not one that is average but rather one that is extraordinary. And that kind of life, this Zoë—God kind of life, is one that requires supernatural, life sustaining power to apprehend.

# About the Author

Debra Jordan, prophetess, poet, intercessor, teacher, mother of five, and wife to New York Times best-selling author and spiritual leader Bishop E. Bernard Jordan, is surely one of the universe's best kept secrets. The secret is now being revealed. Prophesying since she was 12 years old, Jordan has carried the Word of the Lord with startling accuracy in various parts of the world to both high profile leaders and laypersons. While her ministry reaches people from nearly every strata of life, her primary focus is centered on empowering women to become all that God has intended for them to be. She is the author of *Prophetic Reflections: Poetry From the Heart of the Prophetess*. You can watch Prophetess Debra live on *The Power of Prophecy* broadcast on television or by visiting the interactive website at www.bishopjordan.com.

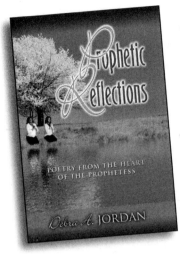

# Also by Debra A. Jordan

## Prophetic Reflections:
*Poetry From The Heart
of the Prophetess*

In the bible there are four basic kinds of poetry, speculative, lyrical, folklore, and prophetical. In Prophetic Reflections: Poetry From the Heart of The Prophetess, I speak in poetry the sentiments of my deepest heart, messages that communicate some of the most challenging subjects that life confronts us with. In every poem I introduce the problem and within the same meter offer the age-old solution—to look within yourself and discover. Unlike other kinds of poetry, prophetic poetry is expressed only through the eyes of the seer. A seer is one who hears from God and is then mandated to take the message to the world. Jeremiah the prophet is one such example of one whose works and prophecies are thoroughly poetical and full of prose. A major portion of the Old Testament was written in a poetical format especially with regards to the books that heralded the message of Messiah coming forth. Even in our modern era, there are still many poets that are seers, speaking forth a message of liberation, forgiveness, hope, and transformation. A few of these poetic seers are Maya Angelou, Alice Walker, Nikki Giovanni, Phyllis Wheatley, Langston Hughes, Homer, and even William Shakespeare. One cannot deny the preponderance that each of these writers has had on society, even in shaping the way we think.

*—from the introduction*

**Prophetic Reflections: Poetry From The Heart of The Prophetess will have an eternal, life changing affect on your soul!**

## Get your copy today at:

### www.prophetessdeborahjordan.com
### www.bishopjordan.com

# Coming Soon
from Debra A. Jordan

## The Power of the Push

## Women's Mystical Secret
of Moving Past Adversity

# Free

## WRITTEN PROPHECY
## AS SEEN ON TV!

To get your free personal written word

in the mail from

Master Prophet E. Bernard Jordan,

simply visit our site at

www.bishopjordan.com

and follow the prompts.

The Master Prophet will see

the Mind of God

on your behalf and he will give you the

ANSWERS YOU HAVE BEEN SEEKING.